P9-BJA-545

A Natural Perspective

ith the
LON

A

A NATURAL PERSPECTIVE

The Development of Shakespearean Comedy and Romance

NORTHROP FRYE

A Harbinger Book

Harcourt, Brace & World, Inc., New York

Copyright © 1965 Columbia University Press

All rights reserved. No part of this publication may be
reproduced or transmitted in any form or by any means, electronic
or mechanical, including photocopy, recording, or any information
storage and retrieval system, without permission in writing
from the publisher.

Published by arrangement with Columbia University Press

Library of Congress Catalog Card Number: 65-17458
Printed in the United States of America

To the Board of Regents of
Victoria University

AUGUSTANA UNIVERSITY COLLEGE
LIBRARY

Preface

The present book is a revision of the Bampton Lectures, delivered at Columbia University in November, 1963, under the title "The Development of Shakespearean Romance." I am greatly indebted to Columbia University and to my hosts who acted as chairmen for the lectures, Vice-President Lawrence Chamberlain, Professor Lewis Leary, the Reverend John McGill Krumm, and Professor Lionel Trilling, for so much kindness and hospitality.

The lectures have of course been altered and expanded for publication, but the contents of this book are still within the orbit of the public lecture. That is, they are not contributions to Shakespearean scholarship as such, which requires a more exhaustive knowledge of bad quartos, foul papers, and drunken compositors than I possess, but a general introduction to Shakespearean comedy. My time for preparing the lectures was limited, and Shakespearean comedy was the only topic I then had readily available. I did not realize, until it was too late to retreat, that the lectures would arrive on the threshold of the year 1964, when an enormous spate of Shakespearean criticism would be produced by our superstitious reverence for the decimal system of counting. Comedy is a topic on which I have written a good deal, much of it incorporated in my *Anatomy of Criticism*, and some repetition in this book of points made elsewhere is inevitable. Still, I hope the book will have its own place to fill. For all that has been written about it, Shakespearean comedy still seems to me widely misunderstood and underestimated, and my main thesis, that the four romances are the inevitable and genuine culmination of the poet's achievement, is clearly less obvious to many than it is to me.

The perspective taken in these lectures is also, I hope, uncommon enough to be of some value. Each play of Shakespeare is a world in itself, so complete and satisfying a world that it is easy, delightful, and profitable to get lost in it. The result is that the bulk of Shakespearean criticism consists, rightly, I think, of commentary on individual plays. The present book retreats from commentary into a middle distance, considering the comedies as a single group unified by recurring images and structural devices. From this point of view they seem more like a number of simultaneous chess games played by a master who wins them all by devices familiar to him, and gradually, with patient study, to us, but which remain mysteries of an unfathomable skill. More important, the reader is led from the characteristics of the individual play, the vividness of characterization, the texture of imagery, and the like, to consider what kind of a form comedy is, and what its place is in literature. It is hoped that this will help him to understand more clearly the relation of his experience of Shakespeare to his experience of other literature and drama.

The title is from the Duke's speech near the end of *Twelfth Night:* "A natural perspective, that is and is not." My own personal title for the book, *The Bottomless Dream,* perhaps expresses the main thesis more clearly.

The book is dedicated to the Board of Regents of Victoria University by the Principal of Victoria College, in appreciation for granting him a year's leave of absence.

N. F.

Victoria College in the
University of Toronto
July, 1964

Contents

A Natural Perspective

I. Mouldy Tales

This book is concerned with principles of criticism and with the enjoyment of Shakespeare's comedies. The principles form a complex theory and the enjoyment a complex experience, and it will be well to begin with some large simplifying device, like that of the dichotomy. We are told, by Coleridge, that all philosophers are either Platonists or Aristotelians; by Gilbert, that all girls and boys are either liberals or conservatives, and, by popular rumor, that all human beings are either girls or boys. These statements are clearly oversimplified, and are rhetorical rather than factual: they are designed to give us some perspective on the shape of a big subject, not to tell us the truth about it. In the same way, and subject to the same reservation, I shall begin with a similar dichotomy about literary criticism. I may express it, in the manner of Coleridge, by saying that all literary critics are either Iliad critics or Odyssey critics. That is, interest in literature tends to center either in the area of tragedy, realism, and irony, or in the area of comedy and romance.

This distinction rests on a much broader one, the distinction in fact implied in the traditional view of the function of literature as twofold: to delight and to instruct. On the most naïve level of literary study there is the contrast between the person who reads to improve his mind or his command of the language and the person who reads detective stories in bed. These may of course be tendencies within the same person, like the woman in Aldous Huxley whose efforts to read Adam Smith's *Wealth of Nations* kept collapsing into a lurid magazine. More highly developed students may reflect a similar duality of purpose. Many of our best and wisest critics tend to think of literature as primarily instructive, or as, in Arnold's phrase, a criticism of life. They feel that its essential function is to illuminate something about life, or reality, or experience, or whatever we call the immediate world outside literature. They thus tend, whether they say so or not, to think of literature, taken as a whole, as a vast imaginative allegory, the end of which is a deeper understanding of the nonliterary center of experience. They are attracted to tragedy, to realism, or to irony, because it is in those modes that they find the clearest reflection of what Freud calls the reality principle. They value lifelike characterization, incidents close enough to actual experience to be imaginatively credible, and above all they value "high seriousness" in theme, though modern critics would have to interpret that phrase more broadly than Arnold, to include a more functional view of irony than he had.

I have always been temperamentally an Odyssean critic myself, attracted to comedy and romance. But I find myself, apparently, in a minority, in a somewhat furtive and anonymous group who have not much of a theory, implicit or explicit, to hold them together. It is much more difficult to say what this approach to literature does when it becomes serious: when, so to speak, it stops reading detective stories and gets out of bed. Let us look first of all at the simple example of someone reading a detective story, and see what critical principles are involved in it. Reading a detective story indicates a liking for comic and romantic forms, and for the contemplation of a fiction for its own sake. We begin by shutting out or deliberately excluding our ordinary experience, for we accept, as part of the convention of the form, things that we know are not often found in actual experience, such as an ingenious murderer and an imaginative policeman. We do not want to think about the truth or likelihood of what we are reading, as long as it does not utterly outrage us; we simply want to see what is going to happen in the story.

The first critical principle we notice is that the most obviously conventionalized fictions are the easiest to read. Popular literature is stylized and artificial to a very marked degree. In the detective story, the thriller, the Western, the adventure story, the science fiction, the kind of love story that depends on the formula that one critic has called the clinch-tease, we know in advance the kind of story we are going to read, and the characteristic features of the convention, turning up at the right places, give an additional impetus to the narrative movement. We find the continuity of reading easier because of an exceptionally vigorous pacing supplied by the convention. Many such stories are accompanied by testimonials from reviewers who were unable to put them down until they had finished reading them. There is an analogy here to the kind of music often played at pop concerts, where a tonic chord is pursued for ten pages and beaten to a pulp for three pages more.

If the general shape and structure of the story is prescribed in advance, then—this is our second critical principle—all the literary merits of the story, the wit in the dialogue, the liveliness of the characterization, and the like, are a technical tour de force. They illustrate the author's rhetorical skill in working within his conventions. From the point of view of the moral critic, the author is deliberately handicapping himself by employing conventions so rigid. The more critically we read detective stories, the more we tend to take the puzzle-plot for granted and appreciate the level of writing that the author has managed to achieve in spite of his conventional apparatus. Similarly with other highly artificial types of literature. If we read a sixteenth-century lyrical poet, we do not look primarily to see what he is going to say. We know what he is going to say: he is going to complain about the cruelty of his mistress. What we look for is the amount of resonance his rhetorical skill can bring out of this compulsory subject: the resonance that distinguishes Wyatt's "They flee from me" or Drayton's "Since there's no help" from mediocre poems that have precisely the same content; or that, in another craft, distinguishes a Stradivarius from other instruments of the same shape.

Of course all art is conventionalized, but where the convention is most obvious and obtrusive the sense of play, of accepting the rules of a game, is at its strongest. For this reason detective stories and other forms of popular fiction are regarded as "escape" reading. The fact that they are less serious than "real" novels is connected with the fact that they are more superficially complicated, just as light verse is more superficially complicated, in its rhyme schemes and the like, than "real poetry." The appeal that popular fiction makes is a deliberately naïve appeal: it tells us little that is credible about the life we live in, and has far less of the power that tragedy and realism have of throwing lightning flashes into the murky landscape of the human situation. The critic, as distinct from the ordinary consumer, may take a negative attitude toward such fiction. He may think of reading detective stories and their congeners as a semi-illicit relaxation, like solitary drinking, or he may reject the convention. One normally rejects a convention by saying that the individual works which belong to it are all alike. I remember hearing myself say this, when I was a student traveling in Italy, about the pictures of someone who bored me— Sodoma or Sassoferrato or Carlo Dolci or perhaps Guido Reni. It would not have occurred to me to say that of Giotto, because I was interested in Giotto, though the statement itself would have had exactly the same proportions of truth and untruth. If one is interested, one accepts the convention and makes the most of the variety within it.

What difference does this distinction of critics make in approaching Shakespeare? The critic interested primarily in tragedy, irony, and realism would probably, in Shakespeare's

own day, have considered Ben Jonson a more serious dramatist, at any rate in comedy. Jonson himself certainly shared
this view. He described the printed collection of his dramas
as his "works," which seems normal enough to us now, but
caused some amusement in his day from those who felt that
what a dramatist produced were plays and not works. He is
never tired of insisting that serious comedy observes men and
manners, in contrast to Shakespearean comedy with its
"monsters," its desire to "run away from nature," and the
like. In *The Return from Parnassus*, a play which makes
some comments on contemporary drama from a pro-Shake-
speare and anti-Jonson bias, it is said of Jonson that he is "a
mere empiric, one that gets what he hath by observation, and
makes only nature privy to what he indites." This is a very
silly thing to say about Jonson, but it illustrates one important aspect of his appeal to his own time. Jonson writes
comedies which, if not exactly realistic plays, still maintain a
fairly consistent illusion. From the point of view of the critical theory implied by them, Shakespeare hampers himself, in
his comedies and romances, by never failing to include something incredible. If there are no fairies or magical forests or
identical twins, there are plot themes derived ultimately
from folk tales like that of the substituted bride. There is a
strong folklore element even in the baiting of Falstaff in *The
Merry Wives*, which would otherwise be Shakespeare's
closest approach to the Jonsonian formula.

In our day most critics are reconciled to the superiority of
Shakespeare, but the Jonsonian point of view still survives in

those critics who find the height of Shakespeare's achievement in the great tragedies, and feel that the romances of the final period represent an exhaustion of vitality or a subsiding into more facile and commercial formulas. My own view is that the turn to romance in Shakespeare's last phase represents a genuine culmination. I naturally do not mean that the romances are better or greater plays than the tragedies; I mean that there is a logical evolution toward romance in Shakespeare's work, and consequently no anticlimax, whether technical or spiritual, in passing from *King Lear* through *Pericles* to *The Tempest*.

Shakespeare will not, of course, fit any dichotomy: I am not questioning his essential seriousness, or the fact that he gives the moral critic everything that such a critic would want. But there does seem to be, in the comedies and romances, a policy of including some features of a popular, self-contained, highly stylized technique. We said that one may say of a rigorous convention that the works in it are all alike. Nobody could say this of Shakespeare's comedies: it is all the more significant, therefore, that Shakespeare imposes some likeness on his plays by repeating his devices. The storm at sea, the identical twins, the heroine disguised as a boy, the retreat into the forest, the heroine with a mysterious father, the disappearing ruler: these themes occur so often that in some plays—*Twelfth Night*, for example—a whole group of such formulas is restated. When we study the four romances at the end of Shakespeare's career, this sense of recapitulation expands to include at least some of the tragedies, as, for instance, the jealousy induced by Iago is reflected in the jealousy induced by Iachimo.

If we accept this policy of repetition as deliberate, we are ready for another principle of "Odyssean" criticism. In comedy and in romance the story seeks its own end instead of holding the mirror up to nature. Consequently comedy and romance are so obviously conventionalized that a serious interest in them soon leads to an interest in convention itself. This shifts the center of attention from individual works of literature to the larger groupings represented by the words comedy and romance themselves, and thus an interest in convention leads to an interest in genre. Then, one finds in any comedy or romance, because of the conventionalization, a number of motifs and devices that one finds in other similar stories, and so an interest in genre develops an interest in the technique of constructing stories. We may therefore see in the romances the end of the steady growth of Shakespeare's technical interest in the structure of drama. The romances are to Shakespeare what *The Art of Fugue* and *The Musical Offering* are to Bach: not retreats into pedantry, but final articulations of craftsmanship.

The key to this conception of Shakespearean romance is, apparently, the word "structure." This word carries with it, in literary criticism, a good deal of verbal magic, and we need to approach it carefully. The arts of poetry and music move in time: architecture, painting, and sculpture stay where they are in space, and the word structure is really a metaphor from architecture. It has become applied to literary criticism partly as the result of a curious phenomenon in criticism itself. As long as we are reading a novel or listening to a play on the stage, we are following a movement in time, and our mental attitude is a participating one. It is uncritical, too, or more accurately precritical: we can make no genuine critical judgment until the work is all over. When it is all over, it assumes a quite different appearance. Now we see it as a simultaneous unity, something that has not so much a beginning and middle and end as a center and a periphery. Criticism deals entirely with literature in this frozen or spatial way, and a distinction between criticism proper and the direct experience of literature which precedes it is fundamental to any coherent act of criticism. The point at which direct experience and criticism begin to come into alignment, in a work of fiction at least, is the point known as recognition or discovery, when some turn in the plot arrests the linear movement and enables us for the first time to see the story as a total shape, or what is usually called a theme.

The distinction between precritical experience and the criticism which can only follow experience holds good for all works of literature. But works of literature differ in the extent to which they subordinate the critical faculty during the experience of reading or listening. This difference takes us back to our original distinction. In comedy and romance, of the popular or strongly conventionalized kind, direct experience is not only precritical but as uncritical as possible. The critic interested in tragedy or realism is closer to actual critical activity during his direct experience. In particular, a genuinely realistic play has, built into it, an allegorical relationship to what both author and critic think of as real life. In comedy and romance we surrender ourselves to the story and accept its conventions; the residual comparison of those conventions to truth or likelihood that remains in our minds is at its least active. But in realism a subcritical operation based on plausibility or likelihood starts operating very early in direct experience.

Let us look at a group of plays incorporating the kind of character who enjoys manipulating others for their own good. In real life we take a dim view of such people, and so, in a realistic play like Ibsen's *The Wild Duck*, we compare Gregers Werle's activities with our habitual attitudes to such things. We feel that our sense of the relevance of literature to life is strengthened when we see the disaster that results from his meddling. In Ben Jonson's *Bartholomew Fair* a magistrate named Adam Overdo disguises himself in order to bring judgment to bear on what he calls the "enormities" going on at the fair. We are further away from realism here, and recognize the artificial convention of the impenetrable disguise, but still our habitual attitudes to life are operating, and the critical faculty to some extent with them. Eavesdropping, we know, is not really a sporting event. We are dramatically satisfied, because of the coincidence between the dramatic action and our view of ordinary life, when we see Overdo going from one bungle to another and making a failure of the great unmasking scene that he has been trying to lead up to.

Now, with these plays in mind, let us approach *Measure for Measure*. We are told that this is a "problem" play, comparatively realistic and something of an allegory of government. Bernard Shaw tells us that it shows Shakespeare coming as close to the twentieth century as the seventeenth would let him. The inference is that we should listen to it not uncritically, but subcritically, comparing it as we go along with what we are accustomed to think of as actual human behavior. After an act or two we decide that, with the possible exception of Lucio, every character in it is insane. At the center of the play is an eavesdropping and manipulating character, the Duke. And what are we to make of him? He disappears in order to leave his deputy Angelo to administer a remarkably repulsive law about sexual irregularity, clearly the only law he is interested in, and which he is apparently afraid to administer himself. Then he returns disguised as a friar to reconcile Angelo's first victim Claudio to his execution. When Angelo attempts to seduce the heroine Isabella, he proposes that she go along with the idea but substitute another girl betrothed to Angelo. A great deal is said about sin in this play, but we are solemnly informed that there is no shadow of sin on this deception—nor, evidently, on telling Isabella a brutal lie to the effect that her brother has been executed after all. Finally, the Duke returns in his own shape, and, after stretching everyone's nerves to the utmost limits of endurance, hands out pardons all round with great complacency.

We consult the critics, and find that some very influential

ones regard the Duke as an incarnation of divine providence. Certainly he does seem to have some resemblance to the popular pious view of God, that no doubt he has had the best intentions all along, but that in the sweet by-and-by he is going to have a lot of explaining to do. I am not suggesting that this is a reasonable view of *Measure for Measure*: I am saying that if we take the phrase "problem play" in its original Ibsenish context this wild farrago is what will result. *Measure for Measure*, whatever else it is, is not an attempt at socially significant realism: it is much more disturbing fantasy than a Johann Strauss opera, but its relation to any actual Vienna is equally remote. We note in passing a fact discovered by Thomas Rymer and at intervals by other critics since: that it is easy to make a Shakespeare play look ridiculous by refusing to accept its convention.

The more realistic the play, the nearer to actual criticism does our direct experience of the play become. In Shakespeare the critical faculty, during the direct experience of the play, is at a minimum. The assumption in Jonson, and obviously in Ibsen too, is that an audience will accept an illusion within limits. How wide those limits are may be subject to dispute, but the assumption is still there: it underlies all Jonson's theories of following nature, of the humorous character, of observing the unities. But Shakespeare simply does not make this assumption. He does not ask his audience to accept an illusion: he asks them to listen to the story. Everything we are told in that story is of equal authority. In discussing any difficulties of plausibility in Shakespeare, we

are often presented with the Elizabethan audience as a kind
of censor principle. We are assured that the Elizabethan
audience would think very differently about the behavior of
Isabella in *Measure for Measure* from anyone today who was
expecting a problem play. But it seems clear that no audience
of Shakespeare, whether Elizabethan or modern, is allowed
to think at all. They have the power to like or dislike the play,
but no right to raise questions, as long as the action is going
on, about the plausibility of the incidents or their correspondence with their habitual view of life. The manifesto of this
type of drama was laid down once and for all in Peele's *Old
Wives' Tale*, when Gammer Madge begins to tell her story
to the two young pages, Frolic and Fantastic:

Madge: Once upon a time, there was a king, or a lord, or a duke,
that had a fair daughter, the fairest that ever was, as white as snow
and as red as blood; and once upon a time his daughter was stolen
away; and he sent all his men to seek his daughter; and he sent
so long, that he sent all his men out of his land.
Frolic: Who dressed his dinner, then?
Madge: Nay, either hear my tale, or kiss my tail.
Fantastic: Well said! On with your tale, gammer.

It follows that the criticism devoted to the vividness of
characterization in Shakespeare's comedies may get out of
proportion if it is not kept in its context. That context is,
again, like the context of characterization in a detective
story: lifelike and highly individualized characters may appear, but we should never lose sight of the incidental tour de
force involved in the skill of so presenting them. Shake-

speare's technique is the opposite of, say, Chekhov's, where the characters seem to be prior to the plot, in the sense that the action of the play is presented as the logical behavior of the characters in it. Shakespeare tells a story that stylizes his characters and may force them to do quite unreasonable things. This is more obvious in his comedies than in his tragedies—the fact that his Moor of Venice belongs to humanity and his Jew of Venice to folklore has much to do with the fact that one is in a tragedy and the other in a comedy—but it is true in general of Shakespeare.

With *Every Man in His Humour* Jonson began a new type of comedy, of which Ibsen and Chekhov (Ibsen at least in his middle or "problem" period) are the inheritors. The contrast between Shakespeare and Ben Jonson is hackneyed, but, like many hackneyed subjects, not exhausted. One seventeenth-century play that we know failed to please its original audience was Ben Jonson's *The New Inn*: we know this because its failure was highly publicized by Jonson himself. Jonson wrote on the occasion a poem in which he scolds the public for not appreciating it and for preferring "some mouldy tale like *Pericles*" instead. A critical issue is involved here that it might be fruitful to examine. *The New Inn* is not first-rate Jonson, but neither is *Pericles* first-rate Shakespeare. Yet *Pericles* was not only popular in its time, but has been revived with success in ours, and I doubt that any dramatic company in its right mind would attempt to revive *The New Inn*, though I should hope to be wrong on this point. Jonson's critical principle was so obviously true to him

that he honestly could not understand why his audience pre-
ferred *Pericles,* and in trying to explain why it did we may
get some insight into the rationale of Shakespeare's technique.

There is something very disarming in the way that Jonson,
both here and in the entr'actes to his next play, *The Mag-
netic Lady,* attempts to instruct us in the art of liking Jonson. He would call our attention particularly to the extraordinary skill with which the play has been constructed. Is
not his protasis logically and clearly laid out in the first act,
his epitasis developed from it with equal clarity and logic, his
fourth act a catastasis or cleverly disguised recognition scene,
where the recognitions are false clues, and his fifth act a
brilliantly resolved catastrophe, where all is made clear?
Alas, it is not this kind of skill but rhythm and pacing that
keep a play on the boards. It is rhythm and pacing that pro-
duce what in Jonson's day was meant by wit, and only wit,
in this sense, can develop parts that actors can get their teeth
into. The last plays of Jonson are by no means "dotages," as
a character in Dryden's dialogue calls them, but they seem
almost mechanical models of plays rather than actual plays.
They have every dramatic virtue except the drive and energy
that keep *The Alchemist* in the world's repertoire.

A play may fail if its plot is too complex to be readily
grasped: this seems to have happened originally even with
Congreve's *Way of the World,* and it certainly happened
with *The New Inn.* In *The New Inn* Frances, Lady Frampul, comes to an inn kept by a host named Goodstock, who

lives there with his one son Frank, who is tended by an old one-eyed nurse, an Irish beggarwoman. The host turns out to be Lord Frampul, father of Frances. Frank is dressed up as a girl by some women who are playing a practical joke, and makes a most convincing girl because in fact she is a girl, Lord Frampul's second daughter Letitia. The old one-eyed nurse proves to be the real Lady Frampul, Lord Frampul's separated wife, mother of Frances and Letitia, and as soon as her identity is established she opens her other eye. This is only the background action, the unraveling of events assumed to have taken place before the play began. The usual enormous and complicated clutter of a Jonson comedy is there in addition to it, and occupies the foreground action. Obviously the audience lost its temper at being asked to grasp all this.

In any art that depends on movement, whether literary or musical, the technical skill of construction is a subordinate factor, and the real skill consists in knowing how to subordinate it. We have mentioned Bach's *Art of Fugue* and *Musical Offering:* when we study these works, we may almost be willing to accept the principle that such technical skill is an attribute of the highest art, because we know that these works do belong on the top level of music. On the other hand, there was a composer called Raimondi who in 1852 composed three oratorios that were performed on successive nights, and then performed simultaneously, all three being in counterpoint with each other. The applause was so tremendous that Raimondi fainted, and was dead within a year, but his prodigious feat appears to have died with him. One thinks also of the motet in forty parts, composed, according to Edward Philips, by John Milton's father, and presented to a Polish prince, who rewarded him with what seems an appropriate enough gift in the circumstances, a gold chain.

It is the contrast of *The New Inn* and *Pericles*, raised by Jonson himself, that concerns us at the moment, and nobody has ever objected to *Pericles* on the ground of overcomplexity. But I said a moment ago that the four romances represent the climax of Shakespeare's technical interest in playwriting, and in one of them, *Cymbeline*, Shakespeare has failed with many critics as notably as *The New Inn* did with its original audience. Samuel Johnson's contempt for the play is well known, and the colossal bravura stretto at the end, where as many as twenty-four different plot motifs have been counted, is said by one critic to drag wretchedly. But although *Cymbeline* has not been and is never likely to be a popular or frequently acted play, it has one advantage over *The New Inn*. In *The New Inn* the action is so manipulated that it betrays Jonson's illusionist principles. We are supposed to take his comedies "seriously," along with all the good fun, as a genuine reflection of nature and manners, and a play so complicated can hardly be taken seriously. *Cymbeline*, on the other hand, is so close to folk tale that the manipulating of the action is at least not a breach of decorum: it does not violate its own dramatic assumptions.

When we see a picture that is a representation of a certain subject matter, we are expected to compare the pictorial shape with what we remember of the shape of the objects represented, and are expected also to admire the skill with which the painter has presented the illusion of those objects. Realistic pictures have an external reference to the outer world, a reference in which likeness or correspondence is one of the aims. But there are also paintings, especially in modern times, where there has been a deliberate departure from the conventions of realism, a distorting or stylizing of the subject, which indicates an interest in more purely self-contained pictorial values. Considering how familiar this is in modern painting, it is curious how little allowance is made for the same principle in literary criticism.

Like every other dramatist, Shakespeare tells us a story and persuades us of its validity as a story. As with every other dramatist, the persuasion is purely rhetorical, not logical. But Shakespeare is not like every other dramatist in selecting plots that are inherently impossible to believe. In every comedy there is some explicitly antirealistic feature introduced: this feature forms a convention that we have to accept, and if the rhetoric fails to persuade us the convention is still there to fall back on. A doctor once remarked to me that he was unable to enjoy a performance of *Twelfth Night* because it was a biological impossibility that boy and girl twins could resemble each other so closely. Shakespeare's answer, apparently, would be for drama what Sir Thomas Browne's is for religion: "Methinks there be not impossibilities enough for an active faith." In fact this is more or less what Paulina does say in *The Winter's Tale*, when one of the most prodigiously unlikely scenes even in Shakespeare reaches its climax: "It is required you do awake your faith." We may compare the assumed name of Imogen, Fidele. Of course the faith spoken of is what we should call imaginative faith, but this imaginative faith is something much more positive than any mere suspension of disbelief, however willing.

There is no intentional fallacy in saying that Shakespeare deliberately chose incredible comic plots, but there may be one in assigning to him some reason for doing so. We may assume, for example, that a desire to show off his brilliant technique led him to plots that were as difficult as possible to make persuasive. But then we notice that failure to persuade is sometimes an important feature of his plots. Iago's temptation of Othello employs some of the greatest rhetoric in literature to make a convention seem real to us, yet, as everybody notices in performance, there remains something unconvincing about the temptation which is unmistakably part of its effect. The same collapse of persuasion back on an arbitrary convention often meets us in the comedies. The calumny of Hero in *Much Ado* is an example; and it is curious how often the *cast* is summoned to a meeting afterward in which, it is asserted, all difficulties in the story will be explained away, the audience itself having to leave without benefit of this. However we explain the difficulties, they seem to be there with the specific function of drawing us away from the analogy to familiar experience into a strange but consistent and self-contained dramatic world.

There are other features in Shakespeare which mark a deliberate distortion of normal experience in the interest of literary stylization. A familiar example is the use of anachronism. The action of *King John* has proceeded for only a few lines when the king says:

> Be thou as lightning in the eyes of France;
> For ere thou canst report I will be there,
> The thunder of my cannon shall be heard.

King John, of course, had no cannon. It is habitual for us to say that the audience would never notice. Audiences in fact have a rather quick ear for such things. Or we may say that Shakespeare was in a hurry, and was unwilling to spoil his record of never blotting a line. The assumption that Shakespeare was a hasty and slapdash writer has often been made, by hasty and slapdash critics, but has never proved fruitful. If we say that Shakespeare had more important things on his mind, we come closer to the truth: certainly the fine image of the thunderstorm is more important than fidelity to the date of the introduction of gunpowder. But it is better to think of such anachronism positively and functionally, as helping to universalize a historical period, as presenting the typical rather than the particular event. The past is blended with the present, and event and audience are linked in the same community.

Such anachronism, incidentally, is much closer to the alleged rules of Aristotle's *Poetics* than impeccable documentation would be. When Caesar speaks of clocks and Ulysses quotes Aristotle, Shakespeare is doing properly what the relentless gimmicking of his plays in modern productions, dressing Caesar in a Fascist uniform or shooting Coriolanus with firearms, does clumsily. In *Cymbeline* we find that the Roman Empire is treated as being contemporary with what is clearly Renaissance Italy. The anachronism is so obvious that, little as we know of Shakespeare's mental processes, it could conceivably have occurred to the poet himself. Surely it would be a more profitable hypothesis to see whether anachronism may not have the same kind of universalizing function in *Cymbeline* that it has, for example, in Auden's *For the Time Being*, where Caesar is the inventor of modern medicine and credit economics.

If we think of literature primarily in terms of printed books, the drama will seem to us at best a provisional method of conveying words from the poet to his audience. If we really want to know the play we must read it, and it is natural for the dramatist, in his turn, to feel that, if his play fails in any respect, the theatrical audience is not as high a court of appeal as the individualized audience that can read the text. This was Jonson's view: his response to failure is that of the author in Sheridan's *Critic*: "I'll print it, every word"; and even for appreciative hearers his feeling is that the printed text is their reward. There they can see, especially in the annotations to the tragedies and masques, something of Jonson's scholarship, which is as genuine a creative attribute as any great poet in English literature has ever possessed.

Some readers are so impressed by the accuracy of print that they feel that there is not much point in going to plays once one has learned to read. Fortunately, most reasonable people understand that there is an irreplaceable value in the theatrical experience. It is a striking and perennially mysterious feature of Shakespeare, as of many of his contemporaries, that he seems to have been so absorbed in the theatrical process as to be largely indifferent to anything outside it, such as the advance in his reputation that a folio edited and proofread by him would have made. His plays bring us close to the oral tradition, with its shifting and kaleidoscopic variants, its migrating themes and motifs, its tolerance of interpolation, its detachment from the printed ideal of an established text. Sometimes we may even be in doubt whether an entire play is a garbled version of Shakespeare or the work of someone else.

This fact about Shakespeare is familiar enough, though it is not always realized how closely attached it is to some of his most characteristic qualities. We seldom think of Shakespeare as a scholarly poet, because it is difficult to relate the conceptions of scholarship and oral tradition. Ever since the seventeenth century, when a contrast between a quick-witted ignorant Shakespeare and a ponderous learned Jonson formed the basis of a kind of abortive joke cycle, the tendency has been to feel that scholarship was something that Jonson had and that Shakespeare did not have, because Jonson issued printed texts with an abundance of footnotes. But this view is one-sided: it identifies scholarship with visual scholarship. Shakespeare, like Bach, was a scholar of the ear. He seems to have used sources in English wherever he could, not because he could not read other languages, but because he was constantly listening for phrases. His ear for a phrase was so fantastically acute that, in using *The Mirror for Magistrates* as a very minor source for *King Lear,* scholars can tell that he consulted two editions of it. This kind of scholarship is in its own way quite as impressive as Jonson's, just as the kind of scholarship in Coleridge revealed by Lowes' *The Road to Xanadu* is as impressive as the kind that Coleridge consciously displays in his prose writings.

I said above that the plot complications of *Cymbeline* at least do not violate the assumptions of the kind of play it is, a romantic tragicomedy based on a folklore plot. Still, it does have the difficulty, easy to notice when watching one of its rare performances, of being a very serious play, and plot complications, like three-syllable rhymes, are inherently funny. They are, however, much funnier when they are incidental, as they are in the setting of a Mozart opera, where we can watch them spinning and gyrating along in a gabble of dry *recitativo,* as they do in *Le Nozze di Figaro.* Plots of operas are often more uninhibited than plots of plays, because the driving force of the opera is provided by the music. In *Figaro* we have a comfortable feeling that no doubt all the complications work out as they should, but in the meantime something more important, like "Voi che sapete" or "Dove sono," is likely to turn up at any time and claim our main attention. Some time ago I dropped into the middle of a Chinese comedy of the Sung period, and tried, with the aid of a Chinese girl acting as interpreter, to work out what was going on. There were half a dozen characters on the stage, all disguised as somebody else. But then these plays, in the first place, had five or six hours in which to get their complications unraveled, and in the second place, their impact on the listener is more operatic than purely verbal. The orchestra is there, providing an emotional impetus for every detail of the action, exits, entrances, even the cadences of the speeches, and keeping the plot subordinated to its rhythm. Perhaps this reference to opera will give us a clue to our present problem.

Only a minority of Jonson's plays still hold the stage: even *The Silent Woman,* so much admired for so long as the perfection of dramatic construction, is very rarely performed now. Nevertheless the establishing of the tradition of modern English comedy was Jonson's work and not Shakespeare's. All the important writers of English comedy since Jonson have cultivated the comedy of manners with its realistic illusion and not Shakespeare's romantic and stylized kind. Nearly all of them—Congreve, Goldsmith, Sheridan, Wilde, Shaw, Synge, O'Casey—have been Irishmen, and one might expect them to have some fey and Celtic sympathy for fairyland, but apart from Yeats (who is not very close to Shakespeare either), the English, or Anglo-Irish, dramatic tradition exhibits a remarkable dearth of leprechauns. The main tradition of Shakespearean fantasy seems to have drifted from the stage into lyric poetry, an oddly bookish fate for the warbler of native wood-notes wild. In the last century, as said above, there was some attempt to annex the so-called problem comedies to more realistic assumptions about drama, but the other comedies remained recalcitrant. Shaw is forced to conclude that many of them are potboilers, aptly described by such titles as *As You Like It* and *Much Ado About Nothing,* which could not hold the stage if Shakespeare were not a cultural vested interest. The only place where the tradition of Shakespearean romantic comedy has survived with any theatrical success is, as we should expect, in opera. As long as we have Mozart or Verdi or Sullivan to listen to, we can tolerate identical twins and lost heirs and love potions and folk tales: we can even stand a fairy queen if she is under two hundred pounds. And when we look for the most striking modern parallels to *Twelfth Night* or *The Tempest,* we think first of all of *Figaro* and *The Magic Flute.*

The operatic features of Shakespearean comedy are an integral part of Shakespeare's concentration on the theatrical process. Thematic images and words echo and call and respond in a way which is a constant fascination to anyone working with the text. Such repetitions seem to have something oracular about them, as though arranging them in the right way would provide a key to some occult and profound process of thought. In performance, of course, they have the same function that similar repeated patterns have in music. As with music, it would take a superhuman concentration to notice every repetition consciously, even if we had the kind of clarity in the performance which we may take for granted in the concert hall but seldom hear in the theater. Yet there is usually so much repetition that, again as in music, even a vague and woolgathering listener is bound to get some sense of design. In the trial scene of *The Merchant of Venice*, for example, we notice, first, how the sequence of events is arranged, not in the order of ordinary credibility (Portia's not-a-scruple-more-or-less point might well have occurred to someone much earlier), but in the order of dramatic suspense. Next, we notice the constant repetition of thematic words, "mercy," "judgment," "will," "bond." Finally, we notice at the beginning of the scene the thematic anticipation of its resolution when Bassanio says to Antonio:

> The Jew shall have my flesh, blood, bones, and all,
> Ere thou shalt lose for me one drop of blood.

Such features as the hidden irony of Antonio's reference to Portia, "bid her be judge," and the emblematic counterpoint of bringing the "balance" of justice into the action to weigh the pound of flesh, are also thematic devices.

The opposite of repetition is the sudden starting of a new action or mood, as the jealousy of Leontes bursts on us without warning at the beginning of *The Winter's Tale*, or as Isabella, who seems half asleep through the first two acts of *Measure for Measure*, explodes into a furious tirade against Claudio in the prison scene. In reading a book we are inclined to stop and look back for the motivation, or, at least, some logical connection with what has gone before. In drama we realize that the connection is there, but it is presented musically, as a new theme or second subject which our ear accepts without explanation. The same energetic pacing of incident in Shakespearean romance makes the use of dance functional in these plays: the climax of the great emblematic scenes in the fourth acts of *The Winter's Tale* and *The Tempest*, which are closely related to each other, is marked by a dance. It is the use of dance, the "concupiscence of jigs," as he calls it, that Jonson particularly objects to in the romances, but to us it merely extends the operatic affinities of the romances to the ballet.

In Jonson complexity is teleological: we are presented with a deceptive appearance that is gradually turned inside out, forced by the unifying of the action to become a clearer reflection of reality. In Shakespeare complexity is contrapuntal, with several plots going on at once and preserving their individual integrity to the end, and with an intricate texture of repeating and modulating images. Before the appearance of *Every Man in His Humour*, a good deal of Elizabethan drama tended to favor an easy-going processional structure, with scene following scene along a central line of narrative. This processional movement is clearest in the history plays, to which Shakespeare seems to have given most of his attention at the beginning, and it is found in Marlowe as well, especially in *Tamburlaine*. It is a form which is very easy to follow on the stage, though more difficult to remember in detail afterward. From what we have said it is easy to understand that Shakespeare should never have lost his affection for this processional form, which is as marked in the late *Henry VIII* as it is in the early *Henry VI* series. *Pericles* is a most radical experiment in processional narrative: the action is deliberately linear, proceeding from place to place and from episode to episode. In the background is the Gower story, with its constant "and then" beat, a story we drop into from time to time when a part of it is dramatically manifested. The evolution of the device of the background from the prologues in *Henry* V is clear enough.

At the same time the way in which the action of *Pericles* is presented makes it one of the world's first operas. Apart altogether from the development of the masque, we sometimes forget how operatic the Elizabethan popular theater was, with its sennets and tuckets and flourishes, its "mood music" of viols and hautboys, its interspersed songs. We are reminded of this when we study the texts of a dramatist who was interested in the musical backgrounds of his plays and gave full directions for them. John Marston was such a dramatist: in a scene from his *Sophonisba* (1606), which is probably earlier than *Pericles*, we have "organs, viols, and voices, play for this act," "infernal music plays softly," "a treble viol, and a bass lute, play softly within the canopy," and "a short song to soft music above." In *Pericles* Gower provides a narrative continuity, like *recitativo*, while the main action dramatizes the central episodes. In the imagery, music is practically the hero of the play: it is to the action of *Pericles* what Prospero's magic is to the action of *The Tempest*.

And just as the structure of *Pericles* anticipates opera, with its narrative *recitativo* and its dramatized arias, so it also anticipates the kind of modern poem where, as in Eliot's

The Waste Land, the narrative connective tissue is cut out and only the essential scenes are presented. Eliot's debt to *Pericles* is partly recorded in his *Marina*, and some of Eliot's readers have felt that the ideal dramatic form he speaks of so often is better represented by *The Waste Land*, which is close to *Pericles* not only in its fragmentation but in its symbolism of Phoenician sailors, sterile fornication, and deliberate archaizing, than it is by his more conservative stage plays. Valéry remarks that in poetry anything that must be said is almost impossible to say well. This sounds like a sophisticated, even a paradoxical, remark, but it states a principle that is familiar in simple and popular poetry. In *Sir Patrick Spens*, for example, the shipwreck is the kind of thing that must be described; consequently the poet does not waste a syllable on it, whereas the dramatic experience which provides the emotional resonance of the shipwreck, the widows' long agony of waiting in vain for the return of their lords, takes up two stanzas. Similar dislocations of narrative structure are an organizing feature of *Pericles*.

Finally, we notice that the dumb show, along with such visual clichés as the procession of knights with their emblems and mottoes, occupies a prominent place in *Pericles*, and helps to make it a spectacular as well as an operatic play. The element of dramatic genius represented by Inigo Jones is clearly more adaptable to Shakespearean romance than to Jonsonian comedy: one might almost say than to Jonsonian masque. Drama, like music and fresco painting, is a public art, an ensemble performance before an audience. The late romances, *Pericles* in particular, are plays in which a union of the three major arts, *melos*, *lexis*, and *opsis*, to use the Aristotelian terms, give us a drama beyond drama, a kind of ultimate confrontation of a human community with an artistic realization of itself. We remain in a center of action where, as in the *commedia dell' arte*, the spirit of which is so close to Shakespearean comedy, everything that goes on seems spontaneously improvised, precisely because its general convention is prescribed in advance.

In his prologues Jonson sometimes informs his audience of what they are *not* going to get in his plays in the way of outlandish stage effects and characters, and in one or two of these passages he is clearly alluding to Shakespeare as a dramatist with more complaisance and less integrity. Shakespeare, by contrast, apologizes to his audience in the Prologue to *Henry* V for not giving them more in the way of spectacular violence. In the deliberate renouncing of spectacle there is something that, for all the reckless prodigality of incident and characterization in Jonson's plays, points in the direction of understatement. The Chinese-puzzle intricacies of *The New Inn* lead us to the dramatic construct rather than the dramatic experience, and the end of this tendency is abstraction. Like Shakespeare, Jonson moves toward a final period in which a technical and scholarly interest in dramatic structure plays an important role. But the logical development for Jonson was the masque, the abstract dramatic construct which communicates not so much the experience of drama as the symbols of that experience. If we were to follow out this emphasis on dramatic abstraction to its extreme conclusion, we should eventually arrive at the kind of drama represented by Beckett's *Waiting for Godot* and *Endgame*, discussions of an action that never quite takes place. Bernard Shaw's *Back to Methusaleh* is a gigantic pentalogy stretching from Adam and Eve to the furthest limits of the future, only to end by pointing to a "whirlpool of pure thought," which would suck down all drama into itself, as the goal of the vision. In such a vision, experience would be contained, not expressed, or expressed at most by a single symbol. We should finally arrive at a mystical unity of consciousness in which music would be represented by what Milton calls the "perfect diapason" of a tonic chord, painting by Giotto's O, literature by the syllable *Aum*.

There is great richness of incident in Jonson, and yet a tendency to abstraction which ends in the renunciation of incident. Similarly, there is a great symmetry of design in *Pericles* and a skillful orchestration of thematic images. One aspect of Gower's role is like that of the manager at the beginning of *Sakuntala* or *Faust*: he reminds us that this is a play, and the effect of the reminder is to shatter the framework of the play and lead us inside it. But the contrast with the prologues in Jonson's plays strikes us at once. In Jonson the prologue, whether monologue or dialogue, is designed to awaken our critical faculties. Gower is an aged figure recalled from the dead, like Samuel by the Witch of Endor; he stands for the authority of literary tradition; he is himself dependent on still older sources, and he is there to put us in as uncritical a frame of mind as possible. The play opens with Pericles attempting to win the daughter of Antiochus, who lives in incest with her father and is consequently his wife as well. It closes with Pericles reunited to his own proper wife and daughter. These two contrasting episodes frame the whole play, and most of the intervening action is contained in two other repetitions of the same theme, which also contrast with each other. In one, Pericles wins the maiden Thaisa from her father; in the other, Marina, taken from the evil parental environment of Cleon and Dionyza to the still worse one of the pander and bawd, is approached by her lover in a brothel.

The setting of the play is not only dramatically but psychologically primitive. Antiochus' daughter is surrounded with imagery of forbidden fruit, Hesperidean gardens, and serpents. Pericles' ordeal is the ancient riddle game, which seems to combine the primitive features of the two main stories of the Oedipus legend. If Pericles fails to solve the riddle, he must die; if he succeeds in solving it, he must die. The logic is that of the Arabian Nights. But where so uncritical a participation is demanded from us, the action cannot be lifelike: it can only be archetypal. It evokes the primitive responses from us that are evoked by popular literature: it has a hero's hairbreadth escapes, a heroine's deliverance from death and dishonor, a miraculous curing of someone apparently dead; it appeals to the horror of incest and the tearful joy of reunions. The dramatic construct, for all its symmetry, has been reduced to great simplicity and directness in order to put the strongest possible emphasis on the immediate dramatic experience itself. The emphasis on direct experience has also reached an extreme form in our day, with the antiteleological, anticonstructional type of music and painting that finds its whole being in the immediate experience of sound or color. Extremes meet, as Coleridge says, and the whirlpool of symbolic thought is not greatly different from the whirlpool of pure sensation in which a single squeak or splash of red paint may contain the kind of experience formerly associated with Mozart or Tintoretto.

It is in less extreme forms that the difference emerges. We began with a distinction between the moral critic, for whom literature is essentially an allegory of experience, and the critic for whom the literary form is an end in itself. This is an aspect of a still broader distinction, which will concern us throughout the rest of this book, between the spectator and the participator, which is to be found within every student of literature or patron of the theater. It is this distinction which is latent in the one we have tried to make between construct and experience, the distinction that makes *The New Inn* and *Pericles* such different conceptions of drama. The kernel of the Jonsonian tradition is something abstract and sophisticated; the kernel of the Shakespearean tradition is something childlike and concrete. There is no need to prefer one to the other, but there is some value in distinguishing them, if only to show that both are always with us, the light and the heat of one flickering but unquenched flame.

II. Making Nature Afraid

Drama is an objective form of art, and we should expect a writer attracted to the drama to have an objective attitude to his art. This is particularly true of a dramatist who, like Shakespeare, refrains from trying to impose any sort of personal attitude on us, and shows no interest in anything except his play. In this Shakespeare is unusual even among dramatists. The fact that Ben Jonson was a dramatist did not prevent him from exhibiting a remarkable personality or from often imposing it on his audience. During a period of personal controversy known as the War of the Theaters he introduces an armed Prologue into his play *The Poetaster*, who says:

> If any muse why I salute the stage,
> An armed Prologue: know, 'tis a dangerous age:
> Wherein who writes, had need present his scenes
> Forty-fold proof against the conjuring means
> Of base detractors, and illiterate apes,
> That fill up rooms in fair and formal shapes.
> 'Gainst these, have we put on this forced defence:
> Whereof the allegory and hid sense
> Is, that a well erected confidence
> Can fright their pride, and laugh their folly hence.

In others words, the armed Prologue is brought in to enable Jonson to make comments on the time and on other dramatists. In *Troilus and Cressida*, often thought to be connected with the War of the Theaters, an armed Prologue also appears, who calls himself:

> A Prologue arm'd, but not in confidence
> Of author's pen or actor's voice, but suited
> In like conditions as our argument.

That is, he is armed purely for decorum: his armor is appropriate to a play about war. There is no way of knowing whether there is any reference to the War of the Theaters or not, but if there is, it can only mean that Shakespeare was keeping well out of it.

Such reticence, combined with such genius, is intolerable to a certain type of stock response, which refuses to try to understand poetry apart from what it knows, or thinks it knows, about the poet. Its motto is that of the critic in Shaw's *Fanny's First Play*: tell me who wrote the play and I'll tell you how good it is. Hence it cannot know how good Shakespeare's plays are as long as it knows nothing about him except that he left his second-best bed to his wife. Thanks to a great deal of patient scholarship, we now have some idea of the order in which the plays were written, and it is possible to write a fictional biography of Shakespeare as a kind of allegory of what that order suggests. Thus the period of the great tragedies was also the period of what Professor Sisson calls the mythical sorrows of Shakespeare, with *Timon of Athens* representing a moment of peculiar exasperation.

This procedure is attractive, because it is easy: one may demonstrate that one is a person of sensibility and insight in an area where no evidence can get in one's way. I think of *Timon of Athens* particularly because it has attracted so much speculation of this kind, and because the critical procedure involved has been so well described by the poet in that play:

> I have, in this rough work, shap'd out a man,
> Whom this beneath world doth embrace and hug
> With amplest entertainment: my free drift
> Halts not particularly, but moves itself
> In a wide sea of wax: no levell'd malice
> Infects one comma in the course I hold;
> But flies an eagle flight, bold and forth on,
> Leaving no tract behind.

However, what was always a foolish procedure is now happily discredited as well. The critical principle which ought to replace it is that there is no passage in Shakespeare's plays, certainly written by Shakespeare, which cannot be explained entirely in terms of its dramatic function and context. We may feel that an occasional speech or scene, such as the teaching of William in *The Merry Wives*, has been dragged in merely to fill up time, but there is nothing which owes its existence to Shakespeare's desire to "say" something. I add the clause about Shakespeare's authorship only because it is natural, when we find a passage which disappoints or exasperates us or seems inconsistent with our own view of the play, to wish that we could prove it spurious.

Thus a female critic decided that the line at the end of *Macbeth*, "Of this dead butcher and his fiend-like queen" was interpolated because she felt that Lady Macbeth had made her peace with God off-stage.

Everybody has his own collection of lines or passages that he would not have written if he had been Shakespeare. I myself long for evidence that the "prophecy" spoken by the Fool in *King Lear* was the insertion of an actor who was not content to act the fool in only one sense. But I quite realize that this is the kind of feeling that a more flexible view of the play normally tends to dissolve. After reading Coleridge and De Quincey on the Porter in *Macbeth*, most people would agree that De Quincey had the broader view of Shakespeare's artistry in this instance, and is therefore right. The coarseness of the brothel scenes in *Pericles* was strong evidence to Victorian critics that Shakespeare did not write them, and equally strong evidence to twentieth-century critics that he did. Here again the latter are sure to be right, as the conception of Shakespeare implied is the more comprehensive one, and the more consistent with Shakespeare's other unquestioned work.

This implies a further principle, that a critical examination of the structure of a play seldom if ever needs to take any account of speculations about authorship. This would still be true even if I felt a confidence that I assuredly do not feel in the ability of critics to disentangle Peele from *Henry VI* or Fletcher from *Henry VIII*. It is true also when there is some external evidence to be considered, as there is in the Hecate scenes in *Macbeth*. It has been proved all through the history of drama that the word "collaborator" does not have to be used in its wartime sense of traitor, and that collaboration often, in fact usually, creates a distinct and unified personality. Nobody listening to a play by Beaumont and Fletcher feels that he is being alternately addressed by two different writers. The most striking example of a stylistic break in Shakespeare is, of course, in *Pericles*, where after two acts of rather undistinguished bumble we suddenly hear the unmistakable roar of Shakespeare's mighty rhetorical engines. But the first two acts, however they got into that form, certainly contain the incidents and images that belong to that part of the Pericles story, and there is no break in structure corresponding to the break in style.

It is consistent with Shakespeare's perfect objectivity that he should show no signs of wanting to improve his audience's tastes, or to address the more instructed members of it with a particular intimacy. His chief motive in writing, apparently, was to make money, which is the best motive for writing yet discovered, as it creates exactly the right blend of detachment and concern. He seems to start out with an almost empathic relation to his audience: their assumptions about patriotism and sovereignty, their clichés about Frenchmen and Jews, their notions of what constitutes a joke, seem to be acceptable to him as dramatic postulates. Setting aside the anonymous and mysterious epistle which introduces the second issue of the *Troilus and Cressida* Quarto, he seems never to have addressed his audience with any other attitude than that expressed in the last line of *Twelfth Night*: "We'll strive to please you every day." His characters may express more highbrow views, notably Hamlet, but then Hamlet, unlike his creator, is both a minor poet and a university wit.

The assumptions of a dramatist or the expectations of his audience may readily be translated into opinions or propositions or statements. If we do this to Shakespeare's assumptions, they turn into the most dismal commonplace. Hence the feeling expressed by such a variety of critics, ranging from Bernard Shaw to T. S. Eliot, that, great poet as Shakespeare was, his philosophy of life, his opinions, standards, and values were bewilderingly shallow. The obvious answer is, of course, that Shakespeare had no opinions, no values, no philosophy, no principles of anything except dramatic structure. Why, then, is there so determined an effort to make him an incompetent thinker as well as a great poet?

The reason takes us back to the distinction between critics mentioned at the beginning of this book. Some critics think of literature as an allegory or criticism of life, hence they tend to assume that any given work of literature illustrates something that can be expressed as a truth about life as the author sees it. *Hamlet*, according to Laurence Olivier, is the story of a man who could not make up his mind, hence the action of the play is developed to illustrate the effects of indecision, including eight corpses. The other approach, associated particularly with comedy and romance, regards the story being told, the imitation of an action being presented, as a self-contained unit. The author starts with a certain kind of story: this develops certain kinds of characters, occupying the strategic positions of that story, and each character owes his characteristic features, the things that make him what he is, to his place and function in the story. The moralistic approach sees him as owing these characteristics rather to his place as a symbol of the truths about life that the play illus- trates. This approach is the dominating one in the criticism of modern literature: critics of Faulkner or Graham Greene almost invariably account for a character in terms of what he symbolizes in the author's habitual attitudes. Such an ap- proach may be more appropriate to modern writers, but it can be misleading even there if it implies, as it is often apt to do, that there are no technical or structural problems what- ever involved in telling a story. If one starts to tell a story about Tom Jones, one needs such a contrasting character as Blifil for structural reasons, not merely to symbolize the au- thor's disapproval of hypocrisy.

In any case, many of the most cherished problems of Shakespearean criticism turn into pseudo problems as soon as the critical perspective is reversed. An example is the ques- tion: "Is Falstaff a coward?" Falstaff appears in plays largely devoted to warfare: warfare of this kind is based on a heroic code involving physical courage and readiness to die. Falstaff seems to be fairly detached about most of this code, and, unlike his predecessor Fastolfe in *Henry VI*, is articulate enough to suggest alternative values connected with saving one's life and retreating from trouble. The word coward implies a moral judgment, and whether we apply it to Falstaff or not depends on whether we accept the heroic code as a value, instead of simply as a dramatic postulate. Naturally we prefer to say that it is not we but Shakespeare who accepts or rejects the value. A tough-minded critic will insist that Shakespeare did accept it and that Falstaff is a coward; a tender-minded one will insist that he did not accept it and that he made Falstaff into an ironic hero. One approach turns Shakespeare into a stupid snob; the other turns him into a dishonest snob. When we reach a conclusion like that it is clearly time to retrace our steps.

I do not think I am threshing straw here: we may have lost some of our interest in Falstaff's cowardice, but we still talk about Shakespeare's acceptance of legitimacy, divine right, order and degree, the chain of being, Christian eschatology, and the like, as though they were truths that he believed in and wrote his plays to illustrate, or at least did illustrate incidentally. But it seems a strange critical procedure to equate so skillful a dramatic use of a theme with a belief in it which was mere commonplace in his own day and is mere superstition in ours. In Dante and Milton we recognize certain anxieties peculiar to their age, along with an imaginative vision that is independent of the age and communicates itself directly to us. Shakespeare's plays reflect the anxieties of his time: they do not show that he shared those anxieties. He may have done so as a man—there is no evidence one way or the other—but it is pointless to make allowances for things that "date" in his plays where we do not need to make such allowances.

The third scene of *Troilus and Cressida* presents the Greek leaders in conference, in an atmosphere as solemn, as rhetorical, and as barbaric as an Indian powwow. In the midst of this conference Ulysses delivers his speech on degree. He wants to get the Greek leaders to try to detach Achilles from his homosexual friend Patroclus, but he has to do this with the face-saving demanded by warrior aristocracies, hence all the talk about the cosmic order. The return of the ruthless and treacherous Achilles will not restore the cosmic order, but it will help to destroy the city of Priam. The audience is not asked to reflect on the state of the universe; the audience is seeing how skillfully Ulysses, like a human Aeolus, is controlling his bag of wind. When he wants to put pressure directly on Achilles he lets go with another tremendous speech on time, to which the same principles of decorum apply. To use these speeches as a basis of Shakespeare's belief, or of beliefs in his audience to which he was appealing, not only reduces his poetic thought to platitude but ignores the fact that he is using it as platitude.

Shakespeare's offenses against propriety have often been deplored: that is no longer an issue that worries us much, partly because we have a different notion of what constitutes indecency in literature. In every poet there is a craftsman who is trying to put words together into a structure solid enough to communicate with audiences remote in time and space and cultural assumptions. There is also in every poet, as in every man, an ego that wants to harangue and button-hole, to sound off and impress, to impose opinions and project fantasies, to make enemies squirm and friends glorious by association. The only indecency known to literature is the exhibition of the author's naked ego, and a great deal of literary virtue consists in the covering up of personal vices. Shakespeare seems to have had less of an ego center than any major poet of our culture, and is consequently the most decent of writers. It is an offense against his privacy much deeper than any digging up of his bones to reduce him from a poet writing plays to an ego with something to "say."

When a great dramatist shows a deep concern for the social issues of his time, as Chekhov and Brecht do, we do not feel that this concern springs from the ego. So far from injuring their integrity as dramatists, it is an essential part of that integrity, and if there were evidence that Shakespeare had such a concern we should doubtless feel the same way about him. The complacent grinning sphinx of Matthew Arnold's "Others abide our question" sonnet could only be another kind of ego. But even concern has the technical problem of preserving the dramatic tension without collapsing into the kind of direct address to the audience that instantly destroys it. It is curious that we can think of impartiality only as detachment, of devotion to craftsmanship only as purism, an attitude which, as in Flaubert, turns all simple life into an enormously intricate still life, like the golden touch of Midas. We can hardly conceive of an imagination so concrete that for it the structure is prior to the attitude, and prescribes the attitude. Shakespeare's impartiality is a totally involved and committed impartiality: it expresses itself in bringing everything equally to life.

Let us now examine another kind of problem in Shakespeare: the one in fact that the so-called problem comedies are really about. In Terence's play *Hecyra* (*The Mother-in-Law*), the technical hero, a young married man named Pamphilus, refuses to live with his wife because he believes that she is pregnant with a child who cannot be his. She had in fact been raped, during a religious festival, by some hooligan in disguise. It was not her fault, but nevertheless Pamphilus feels that his honor demands that he repudiate her. Eventually it turns out that the disguised and raping hooligan was Pamphilus himself. This satisfies his honor, and the play ends happily. Everybody in this play, apart from Pamphilus, is presented as a decent and generous person, even the courtesan, who is usually so rapacious in Roman comedy. The contrast with Pamphilus seems deliberate, and one can hardly see or read the play without reflecting unfavorably on its hero. A juvenile delinquent would have a more coherent code of morals than that. However, Pamphilus remains the central figure of a comedy which ends as a comedy usually does, and his rewards are out of all proportion to his merits.

It is extremely unlikely that Terence had anything to "say" worth listening to, straightforward or ironic, about the society or morals of his day which he was trying to illustrate by his use of Pamphilus. All our evidence indicates that he had no interest in anything beyond trying to entertain an audience with a popular, and therefore highly conventionalized, dramatic structure. This is not to say that he was necessarily unaware of the ironic overtones of his play: it is to say that any reaction to the character of Pamphilus has to be based on his dramatic function in the plot. He could not possibly act otherwise, and therefore he could not possibly be a different kind of person, if this particular story is to get told. If we have a moralistic problem, then, it is not that we demand to see poetic justice done, and less happiness handed out to Pamphilus, but rather a reflection, which has moral overtones, on the structure of the play: What is the value, as entertainment, of a story like this?

The disproportion between action and character is a common feature of highly conventionalized fiction. In detective stories, we may often feel that the person who got murdered deserved it, and that we have more dramatic sympathy with the murderer than with his victim. But the author must follow the convention or his reader will feel cheated. We should note carefully that he does not feel cheated when the convention overrides his sympathies. Yet sometimes, in popular literature, the demands of the plot impose behavior on characters that seems to us to call the whole conception of the plot in question. If the hero of a thriller miraculously gets out of his scrape, that is convention: but if he had to be invincibly stupid to have got into the scrape in the first place, we may become impatient with the convention.

In Shakespeare there are at least three comedies in which a male character is married, to great applause, whom we have been led to think is no great catch from his betrothed's point of view. We have Claudio in *Much Ado*, Bertram in *All's Well*, and Angelo in *Measure for Measure*. Claudio is perhaps the most disturbing of the three. When Hero's infidelity is first suggested to him, he makes no resistance to the suggestion, but merely says that of course he will break off with her if the case is proved. He then accepts evidence that would hardly deceive a four-year-old child, and repudiates Hero in the most public and humiliating way possible. We can rationalize his behavior in various ways, but surely Beatrice has the sympathy of most of the audience when she regards him as a worm. Hero, apparently, dies: Claudio is unaffected emotionally by this, and ridicules Hero's father for taking his daughter's death seriously. Then the action moves on to a festive conclusion in which Claudio is completely accepted, and even Beatrice seems to find everything satisfactory.

The real critical question involved here is: Does anything that exhibits the structure of a comedy have to be taken as a comedy, regardless of its content or of our attitude to that content? The answer is clearly yes. A comedy is not a play which ends happily: it is a play in which a certain structure is present and works through to its own logical end, whether we or the cast or the author feel happy about it or not. The logical end is festive, but anyone's attitude to the festivity may be that of Orlando or of Jaques. It is unnecessary to change our attitude to Claudio, by historical or other arguments, in order to make the play a comedy for us.

The didascalia on Terence's play tell us that it was not played through on its first performance. What happened was that the audience went out during the intermission to watch a rope-dancing act in the neighboring circus, and failed to return. Clearly, Terence was not writing for an audience that gave him much encouragement to analyze character very exhaustively. The Roman audience, we feel, was rather like an audience of tired husbands at a symphony: they simply had to sit there until a certain kind of action completed itself. A prologue to one of Plautus' plays expresses this briefly but poignantly: "You'd better stretch your legs: there's a play by Plautus coming up, and it's a long one." Even in Shakespeare we may sometimes have a feeling which, if not boredom, is at any rate completed anticipation. In *A Comedy of Errors*, for instance, it is clear that these twins are going to meet sooner or later, and we wait for the author to catch up with a conclusion that we have mentally reached fairly early in the play. In comedy, as in all art that moves in time, the first datum is the drive or impetus toward the working through of a certain kind of action.

The poet then has the problem of pacing the play to provide a continuity of interest. The more restless his audience, the more strongly accented the pacing has to be. On the lowest level it must be as violent as possible, with constant running around and shouting, the action described by a character in Sinclair Lewis' *Main Street* as having "some git to it, and not all this talky-talk." But even with a civilized audience vigorous pacing is easier to take in. In music this accounts for the fact that finales are almost always in high speed. The same principle in drama takes us back to our original postulates. The popular features of drama are also the highly conventionalized features, because these latter provide the continuity of expected and anticipated devices which drive the play along with a more strongly marked emphasis. Part of our feeling about the repudiation scene in *Much Ado* is that we are expecting a comic conclusion. The statement "all's well that ends well" is a statement about the structure of comedy, and is not intended to apply to actual life.

We all know Dryden's poem *Alexander's Feast* and the influence which is there ascribed to music. Timotheus sings "A present deity" and Alexander "Assumes the god"; he sings of the fall of Darius and Alexander sheds tears; he sings of revenge and Alexander bursts out of the hall to burn the city. It is a fine poem, and probably a faithful reflection of the cultural tastes of world conquerors, but it is not a definitive piece of music criticism. In fact, one would say that if this is the kind of thing music does to people, music is a most pernicious influence on society, and the sooner we get rid of it the better. What Dryden's poem leaves out, of course, is the *structure* of music. Structure is the area of what Eliot would call unified sensibility: it is the unity which balances a variety of moods, conflicting with and to some degree neutralizing one another. Any fragment of the structure may evoke, by a kind of conditioned reflex, a certain mood or association, like the "little phrase" of Vinteuil in

Proust. But structure as a whole cannot act kinetically in this way, and it does not make for clarity to confuse the effect of a Purcell aria with the effect of a bugle call to lunch. The structure of a work of art makes it the focus of a community. It does not act on people: it pulls people into it. An audience with varied backgrounds, associations, and habitual preferences is drawn together by something that says the same thing to each of them.

Mood, on the other hand, does tend to act kinetically, to suggest or act as the sign for an emotion which the hearer provides. In every well-constructed work of art, not only are the moods, and the emotional responses they cause, varied and balanced, but often two or more moods may be evoked at the same time. Thus the death of Cleopatra has both an elegiac and an ironic aspect to it: one aspect is emphasized by Charmian and Iras, the other by the clown and in a different way by Octavius. Yet we feel that there is a kind of parliament of moods, so to speak: that the house divides, and that there is a final majority in favor of one mood and not another. Tragedy is the name of a structure: it describes one important typical action of plays. It rouses conflicting emotions, generalized by Aristotle as pity and terror, achieves the balance among those emotions that Aristotle calls catharsis, and yet there is a pervading mood of a tragedy which is somber, and which we tend to think of as typically tragic. Comedy is also the name of a structure, yet it has a predominating mood which is festive. Because we are more strongly attached to our own moods than to a poet's structures, the names of categories of structure, such as tragedy and comedy, come to be used in the sense of such majority moods, so that "comic" tends to mean funny and "tragic" sad.

But in literature, as elsewhere, the unified is the opposite of the uniform. If tragedy has a uniformly somber mood, it tends to become melodramatic. By concentrating on mood it also tends to act, as far as it can, kinetically, to encourage its audience to applaud the hero and hiss the villain. The audience thereby tends to break down from community into mob. If comedy concentrates on a uniformly cheerful mood, it tends to become farcical, depending on an automatic stimulus and reflex of laughter. Structure, then, commands participation but not assent: it unites its audience as an audience, but allows for variety in response. The response to dramatic action, as to social action, ought to be a majority and not a totality. If no variety of response is permitted, as in extreme forms of melodrama and farce, something is wrong: something is inhibiting the proper function of drama.

We are not surprised to find that the plays of Shakespeare that are most nearly uniform in mood, such as *Titus Andronicus*, are not the ones that command our deepest imaginative loyalties. We are not surprised either to find that Shakespeare often goes to the opposite extreme. We may have a comedy so somber that the festive conclusion seems forced, almost embarrassing; or, as in *Romeo and Juliet*, a tragedy so full of wit and tenderness that the catastrophe carries with it a sense of outrage. Here, as in most forms of intensive irony, the audience may remain divided in its reactions. Hence both criticism and performance may spend a good deal of energy on emphasizing the importance of minority moods. The notion that there is one right response which apprehends the whole play rightly is an illusion: correct response is always stock response, and is possible only when some kind of mental or physical reflex is appealed to.

There are two forms of kinetic stimulus, though they are often found together. One is the emotional response that produces gloom or cheer; the other is the more conceptualized response of sympathy or indignation. This latter expresses itself didactically, directed toward making the audience leave the theater, still in the unnatural unity of a mob, but determined to do or at least feel something about whatever is presented as inspiring or malignant. There is nothing of this in Shakespeare, and no didactic equivalent of *Titus Andronicus*, which is another reason for the importance of not translating Shakespeare's dramatic postulates into values or opinions or propositions. In certain types of drama the action could be a fable irresistibly suggesting a moral which would be its "real meaning," so that the criticism of such a play could go over the head of the play itself to the conception that the author "had in mind," the play's idea or form. But this quasi-Platonic approach will not work with Shakespeare: his plays are existential facts, and no understanding of them can incorporate their existence. Shakespeare's "meaning" or poetic thought can be expounded only through a structural analysis of the play which keeps the genre of the play in mind as an essential part of the critical context.

I labor this point because it seems to me that there is still a good deal of confusion about Shakespeare's relation to his audiences, whether contemporary with him or with us. Such a confusion may be clearly expressed by a confused phrase, the most common of such phrases being "giving the public what it wants." Any dramatist who knew his audience as well as Shakespeare would know that the important difference in it is not the difference between intelligent and stupid people, but the difference between intelligent and stupid responses to the play, both of which may exist in the same mind. In all audiences there is an attitude that comes to the theater with a mass of prejudices and clichés and stock responses, and demands that the play illustrate them, or some of them. There is nothing to be done with such an attitude except to keep it quiet, and the superficial meaning of the play is what does that: the meaning that T. S. Eliot compares to a burglar throwing a piece of meat to a watchdog, hoping that the dog will bite it and not him. There is also a more intelligent attitude that wants only to see a play, and does not know until the end whether or not that play is what it wants. One attitude is focused on the apparent meaning, or moral, of the play; the other is focused on its structure. One attitude is reassured by the fact that in the historical plays the English are the right side and the French the wrong side; that in the romances only a real princess marries a real prince; that clowns are ridiculous and gentlemen stately. The other attitude does not seek a hidden meaning in the play addressed only to it: it simply observes the dramatic tension. In the final scene of *Measure for Measure*, the Duke has the role of dispenser of justice and Lucio has his own role as a morally reprehensible scandalmonger. Yet Lucio keeps getting laughs as the Duke blusters ineffectively at him, which means that Lucio holds just enough of the sympathy of the audience to keep the scene in dramatic proportion.

Our next step is to describe the typical structure of comedy, which I shall attempt to do in the next essay. Here I am concerned with distinguishing the characteristics of Shakespeare's type of romantic comedy. We have seen that the two words *popular* and *conventional* have some relevance to Shakespeare, and a close relation to one another. We have not explained, however, why certain conventions should be popular: a matter of some importance when we feel inclined to question the worth or value of a convention. For that we need a third term which complements and rounds out the meaning of the other two: the term *primitive*.

By popular we usually mean what is temporarily fashionable, for reasons that can be derived from the social conditions of any given time. But there is a more permanent sense in which a work may be popular, not as a best-seller, but in the sense of providing a key to imaginative experience for the untrained. The popular in this sense is the continuing primitive, the creative design that makes its impact independently of special education. Burns is a popular poet, not in any technical or best-seller sense, but in the sense that he continues and provides modern examples for a primitive tradition of folk song and ballad. Longfellow is a popular poet for the same reason, popularizing primitive elements as varied as ballad and Indian legend. What is popular in one generation often becomes ridiculous in the next one, quaint in the third, and is finally regarded as primitive in the fourth. Various forms of popular Victorian art are now completing this cycle.

The word primitive, however, suggests, not the old-fashioned, but the archaic, the region of origins and beginnings. Nobody can reconstruct the origins of literature, but students of drama have always been aware of its development from, or succession to, certain rituals concerned with promoting the food supply by verbal magic. This primitive element was clearly recognized by Aristotle in Greek, and Livy in Roman, drama, and its memory was conserved by later commentators, notably the famous and influential Donatus. Thomas Lodge, author of the main source of *As You Like It*, paraphrases Donatus as follows:

For tragedies and comedies, Donate the grammarian saith, they were invented by learned fathers of the old time to no other purpose but to yield praise unto God for a happy harvest or plentiful year. . . . You see then that the first matter of Tragedies was to give thanks and praises to God, and a grateful prayer of the countrymen for a happy harvest, and this I hope was not discommendable. . . . But to wade further, this form of invention being found out, as the days wherein it was used did decay, and the world grew to more perfection, so the wit of the younger sort became more riper, for they leaving this form invented another, for, for sonnets in praise of the gods, they did set forth the sour fortune of many exiles, the miserable fall of hapless princes, the ruinous decay of many countries; yet not content with this, they presented the lives of Satyrs, so that they might wisely, under the abuse of that name, discover the follies of many their foolish fellow citizens.

This account establishes the principle that both tragedy and the comedy of manners are relatively late, educated, and sophisticated forms of drama. Comedy is inherently more popular than tragedy, for obvious reasons, but comedy as practiced by Jonson, Congreve, Goldsmith, or Shaw rests on a precarious acceptance: most of these writers, we notice, scold their audiences a good deal for preferring something more sentimental or spectacular. A tradition of arrogance toward the audience runs through such comedy from the Prologue to *Every Man in His Humour* to the Prologue to *Caesar and Cleopatra*. The popular and primitive form of drama is a romantic spectacle, full of violent action, whether melodramatic or farcical (the inclusion of these elements is a different thing from making a uniformity of mood out of them), dancing and singing, ribald dialogue, and picturesque settings. Comedy preserves this primitive form better than tragedy, and romantic comedy of Shakespeare's type preserves it better than the comedy of manners.

It is consistent with Shakespeare's general attitude to his public that he should move toward the romantic spectacle rather than away from it, and that so many of his experiments should be concerned with reviving the obsolete. Thus, after completing the austere *Coriolanus* and the even more forbidding *Timon of Athens*, we can see him turning over the pages of what seem to us rather corny and simple-minded plays, such as *The Rare Triumphs of Love and Fortune* and the hardy perennial *Mucedorus*, in search of formulas for his final romances. Gower in *Pericles* is part of an interest in *trecento* culture that extends to Boccaccio and Chaucer, and *The Winter's Tale* insists on the affinity of its story to old tales and ballads. It has been suggested that Shakespeare was responding to a new trend initiated by Beaumont and Fletcher, but, aside from the fact that the influence was more probably the other way round, Shakespeare's distinctive archaizing tendencies are not to be found in Beaumont and Fletcher.

The educated or humanist view of drama assumed that unity of action required unity of time, of place, of social classes (not mixing kings and clowns in the same play) and of illusion (keeping the action on one level of plausibility). Any exception, such as Jonson's *The Devil is an Ass*, would be likely to take the form of parody. Shakespeare not only ignores all this but deliberately turns back to the expanded screen of the old romances. *The Rare Triumphs* begins, in the convention of the Prologue to Job, with the Fury Tisiphone thrusting herself into a council of gods, and this vertical extension of the action into upper and lower worlds recurs in the oracles and epiphanies at the end of *Cymbeline*. *The Winter's Tale* seems almost written in answer to Sidney's strictures in the *Defence of Poesy* about the romances of his day that show a character as an infant in one act and as grown up in the next, and Shakespeare takes the fullest advantage of the principle stated in the Preface to Fletcher's *Faithful Shepherdess* (c. 1610) that in a pastoral tragicomedy a god is "lawful."

All four romances provide us with infants growing into adults during the action of the play, presented or recounted. The requirement that no proper romance can take less than fifteen years for its total action is met in *The Tempest* by a long and rather wooden expository harangue from Prospero to Miranda at the beginning. Shakespeare had used this device in the early *Comedy of Errors*: if we found it only in that play we might regard it as a shift of inexperience, but when we meet it again in *The Tempest* (and in *Cymbeline*) we suspect something more like, let us say, a sophisticated, if sympathetic, treatment of a structural cliché. The rest of *The Tempest* observes the unity of time so rigidly that the time seems to keep shortening as the play proceeds, this being another device, like the use of Gower in *Pericles*, for incorporating the audience into the action. The expansion of time to include the passing of a generation—a theme much insisted on in *The Winter's Tale*—seems, paradoxically, to have something to do with the sense of timelessness in which these romances move. In *Cymbeline*, as already mentioned, we enter a world in which Rome and the Renaissance exist simultaneously, and the only phrase that will date such a play is "once upon a time."

It is not only in the later romances that Shakespeare shows

a preference for the old-fashioned and archaic. A *Comedy of Errors* has more in common with a primitive folk tale like *Amis and Amiloun* than with what we should normally expect from a Renaissance adaptation of Plautus. Another experimental comedy, *Love's Labour's Lost*, with its make-shift plot, its dialogue of incessant and sometimes vicious repartee and mutual baiting, and the strong sense of personal caricature, sounds almost as though Shakespeare were trying to establish an Aristophanic Old Comedy on the Elizabethan stage, or had been reading Livy on the Fescennine plays of ancient Italy that preceded comedies with a regular plot (*argumentum*). A *Midsummer Night's Dream* takes us back to the folklore and fairy world of Peele's *Old Wives' Tale* and Lyly's *Endymion*, and the matter-of-fact bourgeois society of *The Merry Wives of Windsor* goes in for ducking, beating, and burning rituals of an ageless antiquity.

The effect of these archaizing tendencies in Shakespeare is to establish contact with a universal and world-wide dramatic tradition. Shakespeare draws away from everything that is local or specialized in the drama of his day, and works toward uncovering a primeval dramatic structure that practically anything in the shape of a human audience can respond to. When we turn to, say, Kalidasa's *Sakuntala*, in fifth-century India, we are told of a king who was betrothed to a beautiful maiden but who forgot his betrothal because of a magician's curse: her ring of recognition, which was to awaken his memory, was lost, fell into the Ganges, was swallowed by a fish, which was caught by a fisherman, and so on. There is nothing here that reminds us of the comedy of manners, but the kinship with *Pericles* and *Cymbeline* strikes us at once. Shakespeare did not know Menander, but *The Winter's Tale* is incredibly close in atmosphere to, say, *Epitripontes*, which is so much nearer to myth and folk tale than the derivative Roman comedies he did know. We may say with some confidence that if archaeologists ever discover a flourishing drama in Minoan or Mayan culture, it may not have plays like *King Lear* or *The Alchemist*, but it will almost certainly have plays like *Pericles*.

Ritual acts based on what is loosely called sympathetic magic, such as pouring water on the ground as a rain charm, resemble drama in being a sequence of significant acts, but are not otherwise dramatic. Such acts are normally accompanied by a story or myth which establishes an interrelated significance among them. Literature, in the form of drama, appears when the myth encloses and contains the ritual. This changes the agents of the ritual into the actors of the myth. The myth sets up a powerful pull away from the magic: the ritual acts are now performed for the sake of representing the myth rather than primarily for affecting the order of nature. In other words, drama is born in the renunciation of magic, and in *The Tempest* and elsewhere it remembers its inheritance.

Magic attempts to repeat, on a human level and in a human context, the kind of power ascribed to God in Hebrew religion and elsewhere. God speaks, and the forms of creation are called into being: the magician utters spells or

AUGUSTANA UNIVERSITY COLLEGE
LIBRARY

recites names, and the spirits of nature are compelled to obey. However, drama gets back the magic it renounces in another way. Once it becomes a part of literature it enters into the function of literature. This is to use words, not to operate on the nonhuman world, but to assimilate it imaginatively to the human world, which it does mainly in the two archaic forms of identity and analogy. These reappear in literary imagery as metaphor and simile. The form of metaphor is more primitive and more concentrated than the language of simile, as well as further removed from the mental categories of ordinary experience, which are closer to the distinctions of observation and reason. In its earlier stages literature is closely attached to religion, and metaphor is also at its clearest in mythology, where we have gods conceived as human in form and yet identified with various aspects of nature, sun gods and tree gods and the like. The imagery associated with such gods is magic in reverse, so to speak: the kind of magic that enables Milton to say that nature mourns the death of Lycidas, or Shakespeare that the anemone stole the blood of Adonis.

When I spoke of the importance of convention in literature in general and in Shakespeare in particular, I did not examine the question of how a convention gets itself established in literature. Superficially, it is established by vogue or fashion: a young poet will naturally write in the way that people around him are writing. But if we try to look deeper we have to consider a bigger principle than anything we can derive from social history. The young poet in the sixteenth century normally began with complaints about a cruel mistress. If we ask why, we are referred to a convention that goes back through Petrarch to the origins of Courtly Love poetry in Provence. Two unanswered questions still remain: first, how did it become a convention in the first place?; and second, how did it remain popular for six or seven centuries through so many social changes?

The aspect of the answer that concerns us here is that conventions are descended from myths. The myth preserves the primitive identity of personal character and natural object in its purest form. At the same time the myth tells a story, and the story turns its back on the original magical function of the action. A character in a St. George play may announce that he is a Turkish knight or a doctor or the front end of a lion, like Snug the joiner, but what he will never say is: "We are representing the contest of summer and winter." If he did, the myth would cease to be a story and go back to being straight magic. Yet the bumps and hollows of the story being told follow the contours of the myth beneath, and as literature develops greater variety and independence of expression, these mythical shapes become the conventions that establish the general framework of narratives. Hence the literary convention enables the poet to recapture something of the pure and primitive identity of myth. The myth of a lost paradisal garden reappears in literature as the pastoral convention, and the relation of the convention to the myth enables the pastoral poet to use a highly concentrated metaphorical imagery without any breach of decorum.

To take a different example: *Macbeth* is not a play about the moral crime of murder; it is a play about the dramatically conventional crime of killing the lawful and anointed king. The convention gives a ritual quality to the action, and the element of reversed magic to the imagery that enables the poet to identify the actors with the powers of nature. The lawful king has his place in the "great bond" of nature: he has mysterious powers of healing, and is linked to everything in nature that keeps its rightful place and order. The usurper becomes linked with all the powers of chaos and darkness: not only is his deed accompanied by prodigious portents, but he himself becomes an incarnation of tyranny, an evil spirit that Malcolm must recognize and cast out of his own soul before he can become the lawful successor.

If we keep this mythical and conventional element in Duncan's sovereignty at the center of the play, every word of it fits together into the gigantic and terrifying tragic structure that we know so well. Take it away, and Thomas Rymer himself could hardly do justice to the chaos of what remains. The witches collapse at once into laborious grotesquerie; the passage about Edward the Confessor touching for the king's evil into unctuous flattery; the dialogue of Malcolm and Macduff into a tedious and embarrassing digression. In a play so concentrated there is no possibility of half measures, no residual quality of intensity or poetry or realistic detail or whatnot that is left over for us still to enjoy if we hesitate about the convention. Accept the convention, and the play is all right; reject it, and the play is all wrong. The same principle holds for the comedies, and is even more important in the comedies. When Pepys saw A *Midsummer Night's Dream* and pronounced it the most insipid and ridiculous play that ever was wrote, he was not failing in critical judgment; he was saying what any honest man would have to say about it if he were unable to accept its convention.

The descent of convention from myth does not wholly explain why conventions are the way they are, of course, but it does illuminate one aspect of whatever explanation is given. I spoke of Terence's *Hecyra* and of its curious plot, in which a husband is only reconciled to his wife's having been raped when he learns that he did it himself. The question of why such a story should be told is not easy to answer, if possible, but any answer must start with the convention of the calumniated wife as a feature of storytelling in all ages and cultures. And the particular form of this story that we meet in *Hecyra* is clearly a shrunken and rationalized form of a story in which the original assault on the wife was made by a god, or some representative of one: the story that the same audience could see in a less displaced form in Plautus' *Amphitryon*, and that was still going strong centuries later in such motifs as the jealousy of Joseph. In *Much Ado* we have the same theme of calumniation, but Shakespeare has put it in something much closer to a primitive context by suggesting so strongly that Hero actually dies and revives during the play: "One Hero died defiled, but I do live," she says. Shakespeare's handling of the theme is closer to the Indian *Sakuntala*, already mentioned, where the heroine is carried off to heaven after being disgraced and slandered, whence the king has to go to collect her.

The problems of the problem comedies have to be looked at first of all as conventional descendants of myths. The "problem" of *All's Well* is not any Shavian social problem of how a woman gets her man, but the mythical problem of how Helena, like her ancestress Psyche, is going to solve her three impossible tasks: first of healing the sick king, then of presenting Bertram with a son of his own getting, and with his own ring, the talisman of recognition that, in *All's Well* as in *Sakuntala*, awakens his mind to reality. We may still find it a problem that she should want to do all this just to get Bertram, but that is because we think of Bertram after the play as continuous with Bertram during it. We should think rather of the primitive response demanded of us, say, in Richardson's *Pamela*, when Mr. B., who has been the most sinister and menacing of villains for four hundred pages, instantly turns into a dear and beloved husband on signing a marriage contract.

Similarly, the problem in *Measure for Measure* is how Isabella's chastity, always a magical force in romance, is going to rescue both the violated Julietta and the jilted Mariana as a result of being exposed to the solicitations of Angelo. It is a problem that brings Isabella much closer to Dylan Thomas's long-legged bait than to Hedda Gabler or Ann Tanner. Again, Isabella is unlikely to be our favorite Shakespearean heroine, but militant chastity, which is seldom likable, is her dramatic role, and the condition of her quest. A more complaisant heroine could no more accomplish this quest than Pinchwife could Petruchio's. In Shakespeare's main source, Whetstone's *Promos and Cassandra*, Isabella's counterpart does yield herself to save her brother and gets cheated.

Cymbeline, a play that might have been subtitled "Much Ado About Everything," is the apotheosis of the problem comedies: it combines the *Much Ado* theme of the slandered heroine, the *All's Well* theme of the expulsion of the hero's false friend, the *Measure for Measure* theme of the confusion and clarifying of government, and many others. There are even some curious echoes of names from *Much Ado*: in *Cymbeline* we have Sicilius Leonatus betrothed to Imogen, whose name is Innogen in Shakespeare's sources; in *Much Ado* we have Leonato, Governor of Messina in Sicily, whose wife's name, though she has no speaking part, is Innogen. The former name goes on echoing in *The Winter's Tale* as Leontes, King of Sicilia. The repetition may mean very little in itself, but we notice in the romances a technique of what might be called spatial anachronism, in which Mediterranean and Atlantic settings seem to be superposed on top of each other, as Bermudan imagery is superposed on the island in *The Tempest*. In particular, there is a convention, referred to in the Prologue to Jonson's *Sad Shepherd* and prominent in *Comus* and *Lycidas*, of mixing British with Sicilian and Arcadian imagery in the pastoral.

The same technique of superposition is used temporally as

well, binding together primitive Wales, Roman Britain, and Italian Rome. *Cymbeline* has at least a token connection with the history plays of some significance. History is a prominent genre in Shakespeare until *Henry V*, when it seems to disappear and revive only in the much suspected *Henry VIII* at the end of the canon. Yet the history of Britain to Shakespeare's audience began with the Trojan War, the setting of *Troilus and Cressida*, and included the story of Lear as well as the story of Macbeth. Even *Hamlet* is dimly linked with the period of Danish ascendancy over England. Alternating with these plays of a Britain older than King John are the Roman or Plutarchan plays, dealing with what, again, to Shakespeare's audience was the history of a cousin nation, another descendant of Troy. In *Cymbeline* the theme of reconciliation between the two Trojan nations is central, as though it were intended to conclude the double series started by *Troilus and Cressida*.

The reason for the choice of the theme may be partly that Cymbeline was king of Britain at the time of Christ. The sense of a large change in human fortunes taking place offstage has to be read into *Cymbeline*, and as a rule reading things into Shakespeare in the light of some external information is a dubious practice. Still, we notice the curiously oracular gaoler, who speaks for a world that knows of no other world, and yet can say: "I would we were all of one mind, and one mind good." We notice, too, the word "peace" at the end of the play, and the way that the promise to pay tribute to Augustus fits into that emperor's decree that all the world should be taxed, the decree that begins the story of the birth of Christ. But *Cymbeline* is not, to put it mildly, a historical play: it is pure folk tale, featuring a cruel stepmother with her loutish son, a calumniated maiden, lost princes brought up in a cave by a foster father, a ring of recognition that works in reverse, villains displaying false trophies of adultery and faithful servants displaying equally false trophies of murder, along with a great firework display of dreams, prophecies, signs, portents, and wonders.

What strikes one at once about the play is the extraordinary blindness of the characters in it. Imogen begins her journey to Milford Haven by saying:

> I see before me, man: nor here, nor here,
> Nor what ensues, but have a fog in them,
> That I cannot look through.

Lucius, after the battle he was so confident of winning has gone so awry, says:

> For friends kill friends, and the disorder's such
> As war were hoodwinked

and the gaoler tells Posthumus how little he knows of where he is going. Posthumus replies that "none want eyes to direct them the way I am going, but such as wink and will not use them." Yet Posthumus himself has believed an even sillier story than Claudio does in *Much Ado*. The crafty Queen wastes her energies trying to teach Cloten the subtleties of courtship; Belarius tries to persuade his adopted sons to be disillusioned about a world they have never seen. The word "election," implying free choice, is used several times, but no one's choice seems very well considered; the word "note," meaning distinction or prestige, also echoes, but distinctions are difficult to establish when "Reverence,/ The angel of the world" is compelled to focus on the idiot Cloten, stepson of the weak and deluded Cymbeline. In *Cymbeline*, as in all the romances, there is a scaling down of the human perspective. Posthumus is peevishly and queru-lously jealous, he is no Othello; the Queen is squalidly un-scrupulous, and is no Lady Macbeth.

Imogen is by long odds the most intelligent character in the play, and Imogen throughout is surrounded by a kind of atmospheric pressure of unconsciousness. The emotional cli-maxes of the play are the two great songs of the awakening and the laying to rest of Imogen, and in neither of them has she any notion of the context. The aubade is sung to her in-different ear by the agency of Cloten after she has unknow-ingly spent a night with Iachimo; the obsequy is sung to her unconscious body by two boys whom she does not know to be her brothers while the headless Cloten is being laid beside her in the clothes of Posthumus. We feel in *Pericles* that Marina's magical chastity will get her safely through the peril of the brothel, but at least she knows it is a peril: in other words, there is much less dramatic irony in *Pericles* than in *Cymbe-line*. The ironic complications of *Cymbeline* are in them-selves, of course, the customary conventions of pastoral ro-mance, where the simple childlike pleasure of knowing more than the characters do is constantly appealed to by the author. But there also seems to be a strong emphasis on the misdirection of human will, which culminates in the prison scene.

In this scene a number of characters appear who are new to us but are older than the action of the play. They speak in a naïve doggerel verse not unlike in its dramatic effect to the verse of Gower in *Pericles*, and like it they are a sign that we are being confronted with something traditional and archaic. They are ghosts from the world of the dead, who have been invisible spectators of the action and now come to speak for us as spectators, impeaching the wisdom of Jupiter for allowing things to get in such a muddle. Jupiter tells them what, in fact, we have been seeing all along, that a skillful and quite benevolent design is being woven of the action despite all the efforts of human folly to destroy it. This scene is soon followed by the great contrapuntal tour de force of the recognition scene, when the truth is torn out of a score of mysteries, disguisings, and misunderstandings; when out of all the confusion of action a very simple conclusion is reached, and one which sounds very like peace on earth, good will toward men. The difference between *Cymbeline* and the earlier problem comedies, then, is that the counter-problem force, so to speak, which brings a festive conclusion out of all the mistakes of the characters, is explicitly associated with the working of a divine providence, here called Jupiter. Jupiter is as much as projection of the author's craftsmanship as the Duke in *Measure for Measure*: that is, the difference between *Cymbeline* and the problem comedies is not that *Cymbeline* is adding a religious allegory to the dramatic action. What it is adding to the dramatic action is the primitive mythical dimension which is only implicit in the problem comedies. *Cymbeline* is not a more religious play than *Much Ado*: it is a more academic play, with a greater technical interest in dramatic structure.

A final few words to explain the title of this chapter and to introduce the theme of the next one. All myths have two poles, one personal, whether divine or human, and one natural: Neptune and the sea, Apollo and the sun. When the world of sea and sun is thought of as an order of nature, this polarization becomes a god or magician who controls the natural machine at one end, and the natural machine itself at the other. Tragedy, irony, and realism see the human condition from inside the machine of nature; comedy and romance tend to look for a person concealed in the mechanical chess player. When Ben Jonson speaks disapprovingly of dramatists who are afraid of nature, and run away from her, we find his meaning clear enough. When he says of himself that he is "loath to make nature afraid in his plays, like those that beget tales, tempests, and such like drolleries," the reversal of the phrase is more puzzling, although the implied comparison with Shakespeare is equally evident.

Jonson's own pastoral romance is the very beautiful, but unluckily incomplete, *Sad Shepherd*. Here we have Robin Hood characters, a Puck, and a Sycorax figure, the witch Maudlin, who has the witch's traditional tempest-raiser role,

and boasts: "I'se pu' the world of nature 'bout their ears."
There is a disconsolate lover who believes his mistress dead,
and who asserts that her chastity, like that of the Lady in
Comus, is closely associated with the higher order of nature
which Maudlin cannot reach. This conception of nature as
an order threatened, but not essentially disturbed, by witchcraft is in Shakespearean romance too. What Shakespeare
has that Jonson neither has nor wants is the sense of nature
as comprising not merely an order but a power, at once
supernatural and connatural, expressed most eloquently in
the dance and controlled either by benevolent human magic
or by a divine will. Prospero in particular may appropriately
be said to make nature afraid, as he treats nature, including
the spirits of the elements, much as Petruchio treats
Katharina. In the remaining two essays I shall try to examine
more closely the myth of nature in Shakespeare, and of the
way in which the emphasis is thrown, not on the visible
rational order that obeys, but on the mysterious personal
force that commands. As a somewhat bewildered Theseus
remarks, after the world represented by his authority has
been turned upside down by the fairies in the forest:

> Such tricks hath strong imagination,
> That, if it would but apprehend some joy,
> It comprehends some bringer of that joy.

III. The Triumph of Time

I have suggested that the comedies of Shakespeare have certain qualities that I have been associating with the words conventional, popular, and primitive, and I shall now attempt to outline the typical structure of Shakespeare's comedy. I have dealt with this question of comic structure elsewhere, and will try to avoid repeating myself beyond the irreducible minimum.

At the core of most Renaissance comedy, including Shakespeare's, is the formula transmitted by the New Comedy pattern of Plautus and Terence. The normal action is the effort of a young man to get possession of a young woman who is kept from him by various social barriers: her low birth, his minority or shortage of funds, parental opposition, the prior claims of a rival. These are eventually circumvented, and the comedy ends at a point when a new society is crystallized, usually by the marriage or betrothal of hero and heroine. The birth of the new society is symbolized by a closing festive scene featuring a wedding, a banquet, or a dance. This conclusion is normally accompanied by some change of heart on the part of those who have been obstructing the comic resolution. Tragedy ends in a "catastrophe," and Ben Jonson uses this term for the end of a comedy also, but in a comedy the end might better be called an anastrophe, a turning up rather than a turning down.

To get some insight into this structure, it will be useful to glance back at the ritual forms preceding drama referred to earlier, and to which drama seems to have some generic relation. In these rituals there are three elements of particular importance for the comic structure. One is the period of preparation represented by the Christian Lent and Advent and the Jewish Day of Atonement and scapegoat ritual, a somber and gloomy period where there is an attempt to recognize and get rid of the principle of sterility, later identified with sin and evil. Another is the period of license and confusion of values represented by the carnival, the Saturnalia and the festivals of promiscuous sexual union that appear in early religions, and have left their mark on the structure of such comedies as Terence's *Hecyra*, already mentioned. Third is the period of festivity itself, the revel or *komos* which is said to have given its name to comedy. These three aspects of ritual do not always appear in this order, but this order happens to be a very effective one dramatically, and it is this order that we find reproduced in the typical Shakespearean comic structure.

This structure, then, normally begins with an anticomic society, a social organization blocking and opposed to the comic drive, which the action of the comedy evades or overcomes. It often takes the form of a harsh or irrational law, like the law of killing Syracusans in *A Comedy of Errors*, the law disposing of rebellious daughters in *A Midsummer*

Night's Dream, the law that confirms Shylock's bond and justifies his actions, the law that Angelo invokes to make Vienna virtuous, and so on. Most of these irrational laws are preoccupied with trying to regulate the sexual drive, and so work counter to the wishes of the hero and the heroine, which form the main impetus of the comic action.

Sometimes the irrational law takes the form of a jealous tyrant's suspiciousness, as with the humorous Duke Frederick in *As You Like It* or the obsessed Leontes in *The Winter's Tale.* All four of the romances introduce a hostile father or father figure who descends from the *senex iratus* of New Comedy. Cymbeline has this role in the play named after him; *The Winter's Tale* exhibits both Leontes and Polixenes in the role; in *The Tempest,* Prospero, making a lame excuse to the audience about not wanting Ferdinand's wooing to be too easy, takes the same part in the courtship he has arranged, and Simonides in *Pericles* does something similar. Closely related to the tyrant is the termagant shrew in the house of Baptista, whose father obstinately decrees that she shall be married first. The social snobbery that leads Bertram to despise Helena is both a humor and an irrational law. Or the irrational law may result from some foolish resolve, like the rash promise of folklore, as in the pseudo-monastic community in *Love's Labour's Lost,* determined "not to see ladies, study, fast, not sleep."

The anticomic theme may be expressed by mood instead of (or along with) an element in the structure. Some of the comedies begin in a mood of deep melancholy. The opening stage direction of *All's Well* is: "Enter Bertram, the Countess of Rousillon, Helena, and Lafeu, all in black," and the opening reference is to a funeral. *Twelfth Night* similarly begins with Orsino sunk in love melancholy and Olivia in mourning for a dead brother. The opening line of *The Merchant of Venice* is Antonio's: "In sooth, I know not why I am so sad," and the opening line spoken by the heroine, "By my troth, Nerissa, my little body is aweary of this great world," is in counterpoint with it, though the actual mood is of course much lighter. *Cymbeline* begins: "You do not meet a man but frowns," and *A Comedy of Errors* begins with the speech of a man under sentence of death.

The irrational or anticomic society may be clearly defined in its social aims, like the one in *Love's Labour's Lost*, but the new society that is formed in the last moments of the comedy never is: we merely assume that the people incorporated in this society will get along without undue sense of restriction. At the same time the irrational society represents social reality, the obstacles to our desires that we recognize in the world around us, whereas the society of the conclusion is the realizing of what we want but seldom expect to see. The drive toward a festive conclusion, then, is the creation of a new reality out of something impossible but desirable. The action of comedy is intensely Freudian in shape: the erotic pleasure principle explodes underneath the social anxieties sitting on top of it and blows them sky-high. But in comedy we see a victory of the pleasure principle that Freud warns us not to look for in ordinary life.

The second period of confusion and sexual licence is a phase that we may call the phase of temporarily lost identity, like the wood of no names that Alice passed through on her journey from pawn to queen. The phase is usually portrayed by the stock device of impenetrable disguise, or by the activities of a character assumed to be invisible, like Puck or Ariel, the two most prominent of several "Jack-a-Lent" sources of illusion. In a sense, of course, all braggarts or hypocrites, such as Parolles or Angelo, are disguised until exposed. But, consistently with the main theme of comedy, the loss of identity is most frequently a loss of sexual identity. The motif of a heroine disguising herself as a boy appears in five of the comedies, there being three such disguises in *The Merchant of Venice*. Sly's "madam wife" in *The Taming of the Shrew* and the brides of Slender and Caius in *The Merry Wives* illustrate the reverse process. Many of the moral denunciations of stage plays at that time centered on a verse in the Pentateuch forbidding men to put on women's clothes and vice versa, but it is difficult to say whether disguising a heroine represented by a boy actor as a boy neutralized this attack or was a peculiarly subtle defiance of it. In *All's Well* and *Measure for Measure* the motif appears in the form of the substitution of one girl for another in the dark. In *A Midsummer Night's Dream* lovers are again exchanged in the dark, and a similar device makes the calumny of Hero possible in *Much Ado*.

Other manifestations of the theme range from the identical twins of *A Comedy of Errors* and *Twelfth Night* to the headless body of Cloten dressed in Posthumus' clothes in *Cymbeline*. Some of these manifestations are very subtle and complicated. In *The Tempest*, the questions of who is the rightful Duke of Milan or King of Naples merge with a theme of uncertain identity which covers a great deal of the action of the play. The whole island seems to look different to different people, and the Court Party goes through an extended series of hallucinations. The exact shape of Caliban also seems difficult to establish. *A Comedy of Errors* looks at first glance as though the doubling of the identical twins was merely a way of turning an already rather rowdy Plautine comedy into pure farce. But in this play the themes from the Apollonius story, used later in *Pericles*, work in the opposite direction from farce, and so do the curiously eerie atmosphere of Adriana's melancholy, the repeated references to jugglers and wizards, the insistence on madness, which bring the feeling of the play closer to the night world of Apuleius than to Plautus. The counterpart to Antipholus of Syracuse in Plautus goes into the courtesan's house with a now-for-some-fun attitude; in Shakespeare Antipholus enters the house of his brother's wife with almost a feeling of being initiated into a mystery:

> Am I in earth, in heaven or in hell?
> Sleeping or waking? mad or well-advis'd?
> Known unto these, and to myself disguis'd!

I'll say as they say, and persever so,
And in this mist at all adventures go.

Strained as it may sound, I feel that one reason for the use of
the two sets of twins in this play is that identical twins are
not really identical (the same person) but merely similar,
and when they meet they are delivered, in comic fashion,
from the fear of the loss of identity, the primitive horror of
the doppelgänger which is an element in nearly all forms of
insanity, something of which they feel as long as they are
being mistaken for each other.

The third and final phase is the phase of the discovery of
identity. This may take many forms, but we may generalize
them as social (A identified *with* B) and individual (A identified *as* himself). The identity at the end of a comedy may
be social, the new group to which most of the characters are
attached, or individual, the enlightenment that changes the
mind or purpose of one character; or, as usually happens in
Shakespeare, both. To this singular and plural identity we
may add a dual form: the identity of two lovers who are
finally united. When there are three or four marriages at the
end of a comedy this identity obviously coincides with the
social one.

Singular identity occurs when an individual comes to know
himself in a way that he did not before. As a rule this action
follows the course outlined in Jonson's conception of the
humor. The character is tyrannized over by some trait of
character that makes him repeat a certain line of conduct
mechanically, as a miser is continually reaching for his gold

or a hypochondriac for his medicines. Being victimized by a passion of this kind, being bound to an unchanging line of conduct, is, according to Bergson and other authorities, one of the chief sources of laughter, and Bergson's theory is illustrated by Ben Jonson's humor and Pope's ruling passion. Such a person is under an individual form of the same kind of tyranny that appears socially with the irrational law, already mentioned. The action of a comedy often leads to a kind of self-knowledge which releases a character from the bondage of his humor. This is not necessarily an introverted knowledge, which is of little use to a comedy, but a sense of proportion and of social reality. Humor in this sense is not perhaps a major theme of Shakespeare's comedy as it is of Jonson's, but it is an essential minor one.

It is characteristic of Shakespeare that his clearest example of a humor comedy should also be his most ambiguous one. The action of *The Taming of the Shrew* is directed toward breaking down Katharina's humor of shrewishness and releasing her from it. Shakespeare did not need to live in our time to know that shrewishness could be a perverted desire for affection, and Petruchio, for all his fortune hunting and boisterous selfishness, does display some genuine affection for Katharina. His affection is carefully subordinated to his ruthlessness: if I read the action of the play correctly, he takes the precaution of not consummating his marriage until Katharina has demonstrated her new nature. But in a sense his ruthlessness is the guarantee of his affection. The psychology of Shakespeare's own day would doubtless have endorsed the action of the play, which indicates that a person of Katharina's temperament could only leap from one extreme to the other, from abnormal shrewishness to abnormal submissiveness. We also see the gentle Bianca, whom everyone loves and pities, dealing with her suitors with the greatest coolness and competence, quietly arranging for her own marriage, which has no delays or practical jokes like Katharina's, and settling down to be undisputed mistress in her own house. It may be possible to tame a shrew: it is clearly not possible to tame the demure Bianca. Shakespeare's play provoked rejoinders from other dramatists who reversed his action, but this reversal is already present in his play. Yet even the taming of a shrew is a less simple matter than, say, breaking in a colt. When we first see Katharina she is bullying Bianca, and when we take leave of her she is still bullying Bianca, but has learned how to do it with social approval on her side.

Love's Labour's Lost is another humor comedy in which the King of Navarre and his three followers transform themselves into voluntary pedants forsaking the society of fair ladies. Fair ladies duly appear and make short work of these resolves, but the real action of the comedy is rather subtler than this. The humor that has driven the four courtiers into their retreat is, paradoxically, an excess of wit, an intellectual pride that, extending as it does to Armado and Holofernes, transforms the atmosphere of the whole play into that of a literary coterie, with everyone lost in admiration of his own wit and that of his close friends, and decrying the wit of others with the greatest possible malice. Berowne, though he speaks against the retreat, is more of a slave to the humor of irresponsible wit than anyone else. The grotesque penance enjoined on him by Rosaline indicates that there is something mechanical about his mockery, and that he cannot live up to his own precepts until he realizes that even joking is an act of communication rather than expression. But Rosaline and the other ladies are also caught by the pervading spirit, and the Pageant of Worthies, especially the incident of the baiting of Holofernes, shows it developing toward hysteria, until the news of the King of France's death suddenly sobers the action.

Benedick and Beatrice in *Much Ado* are similarly mechanical comic humors, prisoners of their own wit, until a benevolent practical joke enables their real feelings to break free of their verbal straitjackets. This benevolent practical joke is in contrast to the malevolent one that Don John plays on Claudio, which, though far more painful in its effects, operates according to the same comic laws. Claudio becomes engaged to Hero without also engaging his loyalty: he retains the desire to be rid of her if there should be any inconvenience in the arrangement, and this desire acts precisely like a humor, blinding him to the obvious facts of his situation. In his second marriage ceremony he pledges his loyalty first, before he has seen the bride, and this releases him from his humorous bondage.

The theme of self-knowledge is a prominent one in *All's Well* and *Measure for Measure*, where the attempted descents of Bertram and Angelo into vice are really mistaken forms of self-discovery. Parolles, too, is almost relieved to be unmasked, because the unmasking heals the split in his personality between his bragging outside and his cowardly inside, and he turns at once to Lafeu as a protector because Lafeu was the first to "bring him out," to know him for what he was. In *Cymbeline* and *The Winter's Tale* the release from the humor of jealousy is a central theme, and in *The Tempest* the Court Party is brought by Prospero's magic to a concentrated self-knowledge which rescues them from a state in which "no man was his own."

The most common form of identity, of course, is the form achieved by marriage, in which two souls become one, and, in the piercingly accurate phrase of Hymen in *As You Like It*, "atone together." The paradoxes involved in two souls becoming one are the theme of *The Phoenix and the Turtle*. The discovery of sexual identity occurs when the heroine returns to her normal female garments, but sexual identity is a more deep-seated theme in comedy than it looks. The center of the comic drive toward identity is an erotic drive, and the spirit of comedy is often represented by an Eros figure who brings about the comic conclusion but is in himself sexually self-contained, being in a sense both male and female, and needing no expression of love beyond himself. The fair youth of the sonnets is such an Eros-Narcissus figure, though of course in a very different context, and a later one, thanks to Mozart's music the most haunting and disturbing one in all drama, is Cherubino in *Le Nozze di Figaro*. Cherubino thinks he is in love with every woman he sees, but his love is a condition, not a desire, and as his role in the play is at least half female, he is accurately described by Figaro as "Narcisetto, Adoncino d'amor." In Shakespeare the characters Puck and Ariel are Eros figures of a similar kind: they are technically males, like Eros himself, but from the human point of view the ordinary categories of sex hardly apply to them. In the background of Puck is the Indian boy who, like Cherubino ordered off to the wars, changes from a female to a male environment. In *Twelfth Night* the discovery of sexual identity is combined with the identical-twin theme: Orsino and Olivia are languishing in melancholy until out of the sea comes an ambiguous figure "that can sing both high and low," who eventually becomes male to Olivia and female to Orsino, and so crystallizes the comic society. Sebastian, naturally, disclaims any such Eros role:

> Nor can there be that deity in my nature,
> Of here and every where.

But he has not seen, as we have, how his feminine counterpart has been filling his role for him.

In other comedies the heroine disguised as a boy fills the same bisexual Eros role. For it is usually the activity of the heroine, or, in some cases, her passivity, that brings about the birth of the new society and the reconciliation of the older one with it. This activity takes the form of a disappearance and return. The sexual disguise is the simplest form of this; elsewhere it takes the form of a death and revival, or comes as close to one as credibility will permit. The suggestion is

very strong in *Much Ado*, as remarked earlier, that Hero
really dies and comes back to life; as usual, the difficulties in
believing this are later to be explained away to the characters,
not to us. The same theme of death and revival comes into
All's Well, when Bertram is arrested on suspicion of killing
Helena, who is assumed to be dead for a great part of the
play. Even Katharina the shrew is newly born: "For she is
changed, as she had never been," says the delighted Baptista.
There is a trace of the same theme when a picture of Portia
which looks miraculously like her is found in the leaden
casket. In the romances the theme of death and revival,
associated with Thaisa, Imogen, and Hermione, is greatly
elaborated, and in *Pericles* something of the casket symbolism of *The Merchant of Venice* recurs: Pericles forsakes the
incestuous daughter of Antiochus, a "glorious casket stored
with ill," and sends the body of Thaisa into the sea in a
"caulked and bitumened" coffin.

The bulk of lyrical poetry in Shakespeare's age was written
in a convention in which a male lover revolved cyclically
around an inscrutable female figure who was normally cruel,
though her cruelty was itself a sexual fascination, who occasionally extended enough favor to the lover to put him into
ecstasies of delight, but who could also be disdainful to the
point of killing him or driving him mad. In general there was
a minimum of sexual contact between lover and mistress: the
lover often renounced this or celebrated a love triumphant
over her (or his) death. We may call this convention, using
Robert Graves' term, the white-goddess cycle, and one of its

most eloquent themes is that of the mistress gloating over a collection of slain lovers, as in Campion's "When thou must home."

But in comic drama and romance the action makes for marriage and the eventual possession of the mistress, and Shakespeare is expressing the contrast with courtly love poetry in its most concentrated form by developing an action in which a disappearing and returning heroine revolves cyclically around a male lover, and is usually the efficient cause of the conclusion. We may call this, the movement opposite to that of the white goddess, the cycle of the black bride. I take the word black from the Song of Songs, although Julia, Hero, Hermia, Rosaline, and Juliet are all associated with the word "Ethiop." The dark lady of the sonnets, of course, is a white goddess, as she should be in that genre. The ordeal of the heroine who seeks her lover through darkness, disguise, humiliation, or even death until she finds him brings her close to the folklore figure of the loathly lady, who must remove some handicap of slander, ugliness, or captivity before her identity is recognized.

In courtly love poetry friendship between men usually ranks higher than love for a mistress, being more disinterested and less of a slavery to passion or an imperious love god. This theme of the subordination of love to friendship occurs in the sonnets, where the beautiful youth takes over the poet's mistress, and in that curious episode at the end of *The Two Gentlemen of Verona* in which Valentine, after rescuing Silvia from an attempted rape by Proteus, amiably makes a present of her to Proteus. We notice that Silvia, who addresses her suitors as "servants," and who is called holy and wise as well as fair, has more of the courtly love mistress about her than is usual in Shakespeare. Elsewhere love normally triumphs over friendship, as Benedick reluctantly challenges Claudio to a duel at Beatrice's command, and sometimes friendship between men is made an obstacle to the comic conclusion, the friendship of Bertram and Parolles being an example.

Love conquers all, in general: it also conquers certain enemies of its own in particular. Of these, one of the most important is lust. Love is a specific relation between two people which individualizes them both; lust is an unspecified drive which cares nothing for its object. Bertram, in *All's Well*, is certain that it would be heaven to go to bed with Diana and hell to go to bed with Helena, but in the dark his lust cannot tell the difference. In *The Merry Wives* Falstaff's assault on the virtue of the two stolid matrons he picks out becomes a genuine lust as well as cony catching, and the method of expelling it, by burning him with tapers, recalls a remark quoted in Brand's *Popular Antiquities*, that fires were lit at various times of the year in order "that the lustful dragons might be driven away." Herne the hunter, the mythical figure with whom Falstaff identifies himself, appears to be a kind of Anglicized Orion, a lubberly hunter whose associations are with sterility and the end of the year. There is an old legend that Queen Elizabeth commissioned *The Merry Wives* because she wanted a play that would show

Falstaff in love. Whether she noticed that what *The Merry Wives* shows is Falstaff on the prowl for money and overcome by a physiological reflex at the climax of his efforts, the legend does not say.

As for the theme of social identity, the nature of the new society formed in the final moments of the play, Shakespeare seldom varies the normal comic pattern, but his approach to this pattern is more thoroughgoing. In the Roman comedies of Plautus and Terence the new society is more usually a society of the young men and women, with a tricky slave as their general. The older men are defeated, sometimes reconciled, oftener fleeced or gulled if fathers, beaten as well as swindled if braggart soldiers. Shakespeare, however, very seldom emphasizes the defeat of one society by another. His main emphasis falls on reconciliation, and this in turn involves bringing the happy young couples into continuity with the society of their elders.

In *A Comedy of Errors*, in striking contrast to the usual New Comedy structure, the central theme is the reunion, not of the twins, but of their father and mother. Here as in so many other places this early experimental comedy anticipates the techniques of the romances. The action of *All's Well* never emerges from the shadow of an older generation, the Countess, the King of France, Lafeu, lamenting their losses and living with their memories, and it is the will of this older society that eventually forces Bertram to accept Helena, the conventional role of the hostile father being in this play taken by the hero himself. In *Pericles* the emphasis falls on the reunion of Thaisa and Pericles, and the marriage of Marina is subordinated to her return to Pericles. In *Cymbeline*, the lovers Posthumus and Imogen are finally united, and Cymbeline's opposition to this collapses with the death of his queen. But equally important is the theme of the return of Cymbeline's two lost sons to their father. In the final gesture of submission to Rome, what is eventually going to become the third Troy (the text does not mention Troy, but the pattern was familiar) puts itself into a subordinate relation to its historical parent, the second Troy. The sudden and rather gratuitous appearance of Posthumus' father and mother in the oracle scene reinforces the theme of continuing parental will. In *The Winter's Tale* the central action is the mysterious return of Hermione to Leontes, to which again the story of the young lovers is subordinated, and of course everything is subordinated to the return of Prospero in *The Tempest*.

In *The Merry Wives* the action seems more typically Plautine: we have a baffled braggart and a young man who carries off the girl from under the noses of her equally baffled parents. Yet there is another dimension even to this action. Nobody can hear the name Falstaff without thinking of the palmy days of Falstaff when he and Poins were roistering with Prince Hal. It is clear that Falstaff and his three followers, living more or less as brigands in the world of Windsor, represent a late and degenerate form of this society. Such as it is, the Falstaff society disintegrates when Falstaff is compelled to cashier his followers, and Falstaff becomes isolated from the action. At this point Fenton, who marries Anne Page by stealth, becomes the technical hero of the play. He is said to have "kept company with the wild prince and Poins," and his ability to do what Falstaff could not do, enter the prosperous middle-class society of the Fords and Pages and share its wealth, marks a rebirth of a society older than the action of the play.

The Merry Wives reminds us of the histories, and the cooperation between older and younger societies in Shakespeare, ensuring that the new society at the end shall also be continuous with the one it succeeds, reflects Shakespeare's strong interest in historical plays. In the histories, or most of them, the comic theme, that is, the theme that makes for a reconciling or festive conclusion, is the principle of legitimacy. King John is a strong ruler until he attempts to have the rightful heir Arthur put out of the way: then he goes to pieces and Faulconbridge has to take over. Faulconbridge does not press his *de facto* and "natural" claim to the throne, but gives way to the right of the infant Henry III, and hence the play ends on a strong major chord, with the enemies defeated and the country united. The taint of usurpation hangs over all the Lancastrian plays, but the principle of legitimacy recurs in *Henry VIII*. For there is a "comic" power at work in this play, an invisible but omnipotent and ruthless providence who is ready to tear the whole social and religious structure of England to pieces in order to get Queen Eliza-

beth born. The infant Elizabeth at the end of the play is the
counterpart to the device in comedy of suddenly producing
the unexpected twist in the plot.

In the later comedies and the romances the theme of sexual licence is often expressed by making the heroine an Andromeda figure, putting her in an exposed position where her
chastity is threatened. Thus Isabella is exposed to Angelo,
Marina to the brothel, Imogen, thrown from a "rock" by
Posthumus, to Cloten and Iachimo, and there are suggestions of threats to Miranda coming from Caliban and later
Stephano. This theme also appears earlier: Portia is exposed
by the scheme of the caskets to her suitors, in such a way
that she says "I stand for sacrifice," and compares herself to
Hesione. In the Andromeda story the person who places the
heroine in the exposed position is her father, and there are
several fathers of heroines in Shakespeare who do not enter
the play but exert a mysterious influence on the action. The
King of France in *Love's Labour's Lost*, whose death post-
pones the normal comic resolution as the princess leaves her
lover and returns to bury her father, the father of Portia who
arranged the scheme of the caskets, the father of Helena who
gave her his medical knowledge, the father of Isabella who is
the object of what we should now call a fixation on Isabella's
part, are examples. This father-daughter relationship is
greatly expanded in the romances, and will be examined in
the final essay. Meanwhile, we may note that we have compared the role of the disguised heroine to that of the Eros

figures Puck and Ariel, and that Puck and Ariel also act under direction from an older person.

The greater the emphasis on reconciliation in comedy, the more the defeated forces of the comedy tend to become states of mind rather than individuals. Shylock is the chief exception—not wholly an exception, because what is expelled is the spirit of legalism, but an exception none the less, and one that nearly destroys the comic mood of the play he is in. Elsewhere the individual is released from his humor and it is the humor that is expelled. In the denouement of *The Merry Wives* Falstaff's lust is expelled, but so are Ford's jealousy and Page's miserliness—as Falstaff says, the arrow shot at him has glanced. Hence as an individual Falstaff has as much right to be at the final party as Ford and Page have. Leontes and Posthumus are treated with the greatest indulgence as soon as they have overcome their fantasies; Claudio and Bertram, as explained earlier, eventually become quite satisfactory comic hero-husbands; the forgiveness of Angelo, Iachimo, the Antonio of *The Tempest*, the conversion of Oliver in *As You Like It*, all seem concerned to make the comic society at the end as inclusive as possible. The bad influence on Bertram in *All's Well* is said by Lafeu, and assumed by the other officers, to be Parolles, but Parolles too is an individual with a troublesome influence to be expelled.

There is, however, still a contrast between the individualizing movement of the identity of awareness and the incorporating movement of a social identity. This contrast corre-

sponds to a split in the mind of the spectator in the audience. The comedy moves toward the crystallization of a new
society; everybody, including the audience, is invited to participate in this society and in the festive mood it generates; it
is usually approved by the dramatist, and the characters who
obstruct it or are opposed to it are usually ridiculed. Part of
us, therefore, if we like the comedy, feels involved with the
new society and impelled to participate in it, but part of us
will always remain a spectator, on the outside looking in.
Every comic dramatist has to be aware of the ambivalence of
his audience, on the alert to prevent a sudden unwanted
alienation, as when the audience laughs in the wrong place,
or an unwanted sympathy, as when it laughs too often in the
right ones. Comedy, we have said, is a structure embodying a
variety of moods, the majority of which are comic in the
sense of festive or funny, but a minority of which, in any well-
constructed comedy, are not. Similarly, comedy presents a
group of characters, the majority of which advance toward
the new society of the final scene and join it. But, again, in
any well-constructed comedy there ought to be a character or
two who remain isolated from the action, spectators of it,
and identifiable with the spectator aspect of ourselves.

Of these spectator roles two are of particular importance.
One of them is the fool or clown, who, contrary to what we
might expect, often preserves a curious aloofness from the
comic action. The fool, when technically so, is frequently
(Lavache, Touchstone, Feste) said to belong to the older
generation, his jokes in a different idiom from what the society

of the comedy wants and expects. He is often (Lavache, Costard, Gobbo, and Feste if that is the implication of Olivia's "dishonest") said to be lustful, more inclined to get girls into trouble than to take any responsibility for them afterward. References are made (Costard, Touchstone, Lavache) to his being whipped or imprisoned. The clown is significantly linked—usually by antagonism, for isolated characters do not form a society—with another role in which a character personifies a withdrawal from the comic society in a more concentrated way. There is, as usual, no word for this role, and I am somewhat perplexed what name to give it. Names which I have used elsewhere, such as *pharmakos* and churl, belong rather to the different character types that may or may not have this role. I select *idiotes,* more or less at random. The *idiotes* is usually isolated from the action by being the focus of the anticomic mood, and so may be the technical villain, like Don John, or the butt, like Malvolio and Falstaff, or simply opposed by temperament to festivity, like Jaques. Although the villainous, the ridiculous, and the misanthropic are closely associated in comedy, there is enough variety of motivation here to indicate that the *idiotes* is not a character type, like the clown, though typical features recur, but a structural device that may use a variety of characters.

In *Love's Labour's Lost* there is a group of six humors, five of whom are summarized by Berowne as "the pedant, the braggart, the hedge-priest, the fool, and the boy." In the "hedge-priest" Nathaniel. who spends a scene flattering Holofernes and is finally rewarded with an invitation to dinner, we recognize a mutation of the Classical parasite. The sixth is Dull, the rural constable, whom Shakespeare did much to establish as a comic type. But as the main society of the King of Navarre and his courtiers is itself a humorous society, there is nothing for this group of humors to be except a chorus, commenting on and caricaturing the humors of their social superiors. This chorus role is emphasized by Berowne when, scolding himself for falling in love, he mentions three of them as elements in his own mind:

> A critic, nay, a night-watch constable,
> A domineering pedant o'er the boy.

Of these six humors, the central fool or clown role is taken by Costard and the central *idiotes* role by Armado. Both of these extend, by caricature, the verbal play that is the main subject of this comedy. Costard is delighted with the display of verbal agility he hears around him, and says:

O' my troth, most sweet jests! most incony vulgar wit!
When it comes so smoothly off, so obscenely, as it were, so fit.

But, as often happens with Shakespeare's clowns, his own attempts to take part in the verbal repartee are not too successful. His enthusiasm is all the more generous in that he has just been sharply rebuked by the ladies for not being obscene in an upper-class way, as they are.

Armado, who for a conventional braggart with a Spanish name recalling "Armada" is a curiously gentle and wistful figure, starts out as the butt of the courtiers. But his grandiloquent language proceeds from the love of his own wit, and his love of his own wit, as I have previously tried to explain, is no more ridiculous than theirs. He and Costard are, as is so often true of the clown and the *idiotes*, linked by antagonism: they are rivals for the same girl, and a quarrel breaks out between them. But when the action is sobered by the news of the death of the King of France, Armado moves to the center of the stage. It is he who takes on the full three-year vow of loyalty to a cause which the four courtiers have dispensed with so easily; he who is master of ceremonies during the beautiful and muted conclusion, and he who dismisses the cast almost with a benediction: "You that way; we this way."

In *As You Like It* the clown is Touchstone and the *idiotes* Jaques. Jaques is a wanderer, the Italianate traveler so often ridiculed in Elizabethan literature: he is a sentimentalist and a melancholic. He is fascinated by Touchstone, feels a sense of kinship with him, and attempts to become a satirist, practicing on Orlando and Rosalind with very little success. Clearly, he is a Childe Harold but no Byron. We notice too his jealousy of Touchstone and his dislike of seeing Touchstone marry Audrey and take part in the festive society. In *Twelfth Night* the clown is Feste and the *idiotes* Malvolio, and here again is the link of antagonism. Feste is ridiculed by Malvolio as a stale clown, and in revenge forces Malvolio into a clown role. When Olivia says to Malvolio "Alas, poor fool, how have they baffled thee!" the application of the word "fool" to Malvolio is a signal for Feste to mark the completion of the action by his reference to the whirligig of time.

In *The Taming of the Shrew* the clown is Christopher Sly, who is also the spectator of the rest of the play. In the play we know he falls asleep after a few lines, which is more consistent both with his nature and with the unity of the action. But in the alternative version, *The Taming of a Shrew*, the entire action is presented to him as a wish-fulfillment dream: he describes it as the best dream that ever he had in his life, and goes off at the end to apply its principles to Mrs. Sly. The audience is clearly not expected to be sanguine about his success, so that he has a kind of embryonic and anticipatory *idiotes* role as well. In *The Merry Wives* Falstaff has both roles, but even when united in the same person they are still at loggerheads with each other: Falstaff is continually wondering how so intelligent a person as himself can be such a dupe.

In *All's Well* Lavache is the clown and Parolles, like Falstaff and Malvolio, is the *idiotes* as butt or gull. As usual, there are sharp exchanges of antagonism between them, but there is so much of the clown in Parolles and so much of the sardonic misanthropic *idiotes* in the "shrewd and unhappy" Lavache that the two roles seem at times to interchange. In *Measure for Measure* Lucio is another compulsive talker like Parolles, but Parolles is able to observe his own compulsions, and his exposure brings him to a terrifying flash of self-enlightenment: "Simply the thing I am/Shall make me live." There is nothing of this capacity for self-discovery in Lucio. His refusal to bail Pompey, who has something of an abortive clown role, is in the customary pattern of antagonism:

otherwise, Lucio is a clown rather than an *idiotes*. The Duke's command to him to marry the whore he has made pregnant, in defiance of his own comfortable standard in such matters, again associates him with the typical lustful clown.

In *The Merchant of Venice* the clown is Gobbo and the *idiotes* Shylock, who is also misanthropic and opposed to festivity on principle. The link of antagonism between the two is slight but significant: Gobbo's desertion of Shylock for Bassanio is an anticipation of the elopement of Jessica and the transfer of social power from Shylock to the Bassanio group. The *idiotes* is again sinister in the misanthropic Don John of *Much Ado*, although Beatrice pretends that Benedick has both roles when she says of him (and to him in disguise): "He is the Prince's jester: a very dull fool; only his gift is in devising impossible slanders." In this play the clown, Dogberry, is a malappropriate constable in the tradition of Dull. In the romances the fact that characters tend to assume a place in a definite moral hierarchy changes the emphasis of these two roles, in a way we shall examine later. In Caliban the *idiotes* is identified with the natural man, the human creature who has nature but no nurture, and who, like Swift's Yahoo, demonstrates that human nature as such is not capable of forming a society. Caliban, however, joins, not the villains, Antonio and Sebastian, but the clowns Stephano and Trinculo, of whom Trinculo is a professional jester, and here again Caliban's immediate and violent jealousy of Trinculo follows the usual pattern.

In tragedy, of course, the hero is always something of an *idiotes*, isolated from the society in which he has his being. Perhaps the most concentrated study of social isolation in the tragedies is *Coriolanus*, where the hero is a man whose "heart's his mouth," who, like Moliere's Alceste in a comic setting, carries sincerity to the extreme of a social vice. In Plutarch the Greek counterpart, or rather contrast, to Coriolanus is Alcibiades, who also returns in revenge to the city that has exiled him, and it would be a logical development for Shakespeare to go from the isolation of Coriolanus to the isolation of Alcibiades's friend Timon. It may seem an irresponsible paradox to speak of *Timon of Athens* as a comedy. Yet if we think of it simply as a tragedy, we are almost bound to see it as a failed tragedy, comparing it to its disadvantage with *King Lear*. But we can hardly suppose that Shakespeare was foolish enough to attempt the same kind of thing that he attempted in *King Lear* with so middle-class and un-titanic a hero. It seems to me that this extraordinary play, half morality and half folk tale, the fourth and last of the Plutarchan plays, is the logical transition from *Coriolanus* to the romances, and that it has many features making for an *idiotes* comedy rather than a tragedy. If we were to see the action of *Twelfth Night* through the eyes of the madly used Malvolio, or the action of *The Merchant of Venice* through the eyes of the bankrupt and beggared Shylock, the tone would not be greatly different from that of the second half of *Timon of Athens*.

In the first half of this play Timon is surrounded by the
rare triumphs of love and fortune, for a masque of Cupid in
his honor takes place at his banquet and his painter depicts
him as under the favor of fortune. It gradually dawns on us
that what seems to be generosity is rather, or is also, a humor
of prodigality. Timon is never released from his humor; the
humor merely goes into reverse, and in his exile he keeps
flinging gold at his visitors from opposite motives. His story
is, in the words of Launce, a parable of the prodigious son
who has spent his proportion, but he is as prodigal with
curses as blessings, and his misanthropy represents as much
of a social half-truth as his benevolence did before. The fact
that there is no heroine in this play, nor in fact any females
at all except a brace of whores attached to Alcibiades, reinforces the sense of the play as a comedy of humor with no
focus for a comic development.

In the festive society of Timon's prosperous days the *idiotes* is Apemantus. Apemantus is something of a clown too,
but the *idiotes* is normally higher in social rank than the
clown, and Apemantus carries a fool around with him partly
to make this point. Apemantus is, like Jaques, a philosopher,
of the Cynic school, though his ideal is the Stoic one of
invulnerability, as his name, which means "suffering no
pain," signifies. After Timon becomes a misanthrope, he
takes over the *idiotes* role, and Apemantus comes to visit him
and point out that his motivation is suspect. From the point
of view of comic structure, what he is really protesting about

is being himself degraded to the rank of clown as Timon becomes the *idiotes*. In the quarrel that ensues between them, each is trying to assert that the other is really a fool and not a genuine misanthrope.

These examples of alienated characters in Shakespearean comedy will enable us to understand some of the things that Shakespeare does with them. The most obvious, of course, is to vary the tone and express through these characters what I have called the minority moods of the play. A more important use of them is to give a new dimension to the perspective of the play. I have spoken of the member of the audience as being both participant and spectator of the action, but the same thing is *a fortiori* true of the author, who has both to create and to observe his creation. The clown and *idiotes* have a curious but consistent relationship to the making of the play as well as to the seeing of it. There is an association between being a clown and being on the stage, the clown, when fool, being professionally a dramatic figure, or motley to the view. In two plays, *Love's Labour's Lost* and *A Midsummer Night's Dream*, a group of six clowns put on a play of their own, and in one, *The Taming of the Shrew*, the clown is an audience in himself. We notice too that the *idiotes* is often a rhetorician, and that he frequently delivers a set speech, like the speech on the seven ages of man in *As You Like It*. Just as Duke Senior's "sermons in stones" speech establishes the moral reality that keeps the pastoral convention alive in literature, so this speech, by looking at human life in terms of theatrical illusion, establishes, as in a

mirror, the reality of experience that theatrical illusion provides. It is thus the imaginative focus of a highly artificial
comedy, where the sense of a show being put on never disappears from the action, and is not intended to do so.

What fascinates us about the *idiotes* and clown is that
they are not purely isolated individuals: we get fitful glimpses
of a hidden world which they guard or symbolize. They may
be able to speak for their world, like Jaques, or it may remain
locked up in their minds, breaking through suddenly and
involuntarily. The world we glimpse may be evil, like Don
John's cave of spleen, or ridiculous, like the world of Malvolio's fantasies which are, in Olivia's parody of the Song of
Songs, sick of self-love. But it is never a wholly simple world,
and it exerts on the main action a force which is either
counterdramatic or antidramatic. Some of the most haunting
speeches in Shakespeare are connected with these shifts of
perspective provided by alienated characters. What often
happens is that something external to us is suddenly internalized, so that we are forced to participate in what we have
been conditioned to think of as removed from us and our
sympathies. Shylock's "Hath not a Jew" speech comes to
mind, with its disconcerting and unreasonable reminder that
a stage-villain Jew may have learned his villainy from a Christian society.

And yet the primary reason for such shifts of perspective is
not to gain our sympathy for such characters. We may understand this better from the analogy of tragedy. In tragedy
we recognize the importance of catharsis: pity, like terror, is

raised, but it is ultimately set aside. In watching the ups and downs of York and Lancaster in the *Henry VI* plays we feel an automatic sympathy for the losers, qualified by all the evidence that one side is no less cruel and revengeful than the other. The losers are humanly vulnerable in a way that the winners are not. But sympathy for them, while it may be morally superior to contempt for them, would still coarsen and blunt the dramatic point. The dramatic point is tragic, and tragedy presents the event: this happens, whatever our feelings or moral reflections about it may be. If we ask why tragedy's presentation of this event is important, the answer takes us back to the myth of tragedy. Pity and terror are moral reflections about the tragic characters, and tragedy is not dependent on moral qualities. The tragic hero, whether a good or a bad man in himself, is isolated by the tragic action from his community: his fall, while it destroys him, invisibly reintegrates him with the community of the audience. As long as he was in prosperity he was inscrutable, with his own world locked up inside him; once fallen, something of his world passes into our possession, as in the original rite his blood and body are supposed to have done.

Comedy, like tragedy, has its catharsis, sympathy and ridicule being what correspond to pity and terror in tragedy. The action of *The Merchant of Venice* moves from justice to mercy, and mercy is not opposed to justice, but is an authority which contains or internalizes justice. The justice of Shylock's bond is external, and the fall of Shylock is part of the process of internalizing justice: this is a point we shall return to in the final essay. To regard Shylock ultimately either with sympathy or with contempt is a response of mood only: either attitude would keep him externalized. Shylock is the focus of the comic catharsis of the play because both moods are relevant to him. We feel the possibility of both, but neither is the comic point of Shylock's role.

We approach nearer to this comic point when we recognize the strength of the dramatic tension between Shylock and the rest of the play. The sense of festivity, which corresponds to pity in tragedy, is always present at the end of a romantic comedy. This takes the form of a party, usually a wedding, in which we feel, to some degree, participants. We are invited to the festivity and we put the best face we can on whatever feelings we may still have about the recent behavior of some of the characters, often including the bridegroom. In Shakespeare the new society is remarkably catholic in its tolerance; but there is always a part of us that remains a spectator, detached and observant, aware of other nuances and values. This sense of alienation, which in tragedy is terror, is almost bound to be represented by somebody or something in the play, and even if, like Shylock, he disappears in the fourth act, we never quite forget him. We seldom consciously feel identified with him, for he himself wants no such identification: we may even hate or despise him, but he is there, the eternal questioning Satan who is still not quite silenced by the vindication of Job. Part of us is at the wedding feast applauding the loud bassoon; part of us is still out in the street hypnotized by some graybeard loon and listening to a wild tale of guilt and loneliness and injustice and mysterious revenge. There seems no way of reconciling these two things. Participation and detachment, sympathy and ridicule, sociability and isolation, are inseparable in the complex we call comedy, a complex that is begotten by the paradox of life itself, in which merely to exist is both to be a part of something else and yet never to be a part of it, and in which all freedom and joy are inseparably a belonging and an escape.

But whenever we run into an insoluble paradox in Shakespeare, there is usually one more step to take. Tragic and comic structures move horizontally across the action, and appeal to the participant in us. The overthrow of the anti-comic power has about it some feeling of a Saturnalia, or reversal of the social order to something closer to the Golden Age. Such a reversal does not (at any rate not in Shakespeare) alter the actual hierarchy of society. Kings remain kings, and clowns clowns: only the personal relations within the society are altered. But there can be another kind of movement at right angles, so to speak, to the other, one which appeals to us as spectators rather than participants, and comes to us through a spectator character. This spectator response may be one of a number of moods, and so merely suggest additional emotional responses. But occasionally such a character may speak to a focused mood which gets past the conflict of sympathy and ridicule, and becomes a direct insight into the comic catharsis itself. Such responses are bound to be brief, as participating experiences, but they have a penetrating quality out of all proportion to their duration.

The clown is a convenient focus for this kind of response because he is a character who devotes himself to being ridiculous, and hence very readily becomes pathetic as well, thus setting up the two Herculean pillars we have to pass through to further knowledge. In *All's Well* the clown Lavache, the most mirthless even of Shakespeare's clowns, makes a speech that seems utterly remote from the action, even as a commentary on it:

I am a woodland fellow, sir, that always loved a great fire; and the master I speak of ever keeps a good fire. But sure, he is the prince of the world: let his nobility remain in's court. I am for the house with the narrow gate, which I take to be too little for pomp to enter: some that humble themselves may, but the many will be too chill and tender, and they'll be for the flowery way that leads to the broad gate and the great fire.

Lavache is simply an old clown who has nothing left him but the privilege of uninhibited speech. Uninhibited speech ought to be witty, on Freudian principles, but if it fails to be that it may still be oracular, a quality close to wit, and often used by Shakespeare instead of it. As we listen to Lavache the play begins to recede until we find ourselves looking, not at a sullen Bertram being dragged kicking and screaming into a happy marriage, but at the mass of humanity moving witlessly, like lemmings, to its own annihilation. The point of the speech is structural: it sums up the blind and deluded movement that sent Bertram out to the wars, and anticipates the completion of the action by which Helena brings him home again, in opposition to everything he thinks he wants. *All's Well* is unusual in that Helena is inferior in social status to Bertram (or at least that is Bertram's view), hence there is an additional point in this sudden glimpse, very rare in Shakespeare, of the greater Saturnalia suggested in the Gospels in which the social ranks of this world are reversed in another.

Again, here is Dromio of Ephesus in *A Comedy of Errors*, after he has been repeatedly beaten and called an ass:

I am an ass indeed; you may prove it by my long ears. I have served him from the hour of my nativity to this instant, and have nothing at his hands for my service but blows. When I am cold, he heats me with beating; when I am warm, he cools me with beating. I am waked with it when I sleep, raised with it when I set, driven out of doors with it when I go from home, welcomed home with it when I return: nay, I bear it on my shoulders, as a beggar wont her brat; and, I think, when he hath lamed me, I shall beg with it from door to door.

The word "ass," so often used in this play, reminds us of Apuleius. "If thou art changed to aught, 'tis to an ass," Luciana says to the other Dromio. Here, as in Apuleius, we get a glimpse of what the human world would look like to a conscious ass: an inferno of malignant and purposeless beating. But the primary reason for this speech is not to rouse sympathy for the servant, though this is a secondary reason, and relevant to the context. The primary reason, again, is structural. The structure of *A Comedy of Errors* is a metamorphosis structure, a descent into illusion and an emer-

gence into recognition. The main action takes place in a
world of illusion and assumed madness; the imagery of the
final recognition scene suggests a passing through death into
a new world. Not only is Aegeon delivered from death at the
very moment of his execution, but the Ephesus twins are
imprisoned "in a dark and dankish vault," by "a living dead
man" with no face. They escape by gnawing through their
bonds, and the symbolism of this is at once pounced on by
Dromio of Ephesus:

> Within this hour I was his bondman, sir,
> But he, I thank him, gnawed in two my cords:
> Now am I Dromio, and his man unbound.

The Duke's remark, "I think you all have drunk of Circe's
cup," and his comment when the twins meet, "One of these
men is Genius to the other," fill out the same metamorphosis
pattern. In Apuleius the descent into illusion is symbolized
by the metamorphosis of Lucius into an ass, the ascent to
reality by release from this shape through the power of Isis:
we may compare the role of Diana in *Pericles*, which uses the
same Ephesian setting for its conclusion. The speech of
Dromio of Ephesus quoted above recalls the Apuleian
theme, and so is counterpoint in contrary motion to the final
deliverance.

The word "ass" is often applied to the clown in Shakespeare, especially in *Twelfth Night* and *Much Ado*, but the
theme of metamorphosis into an ass takes us to *A Midsummer Night's Dream*. Bottom, like Sly, is raised by what

seems a rather heartless practical joke from a fool's world to a prince's. In the *cognitio* the four lovers and Bottom are awakened out of a trance "more dead/Than common sleep." The trance causes little comment from the lovers, who have nothing to do but marry each other, and as far as the Quince company is concerned Bottom says nothing but "Not a word of me." From Heraclitus, who says that in dreams every man is his own Logos, to Freud, who says that every dream has a point at which it is unfathomable, a link with the unknown, it has been recognized that a dream is the heart of the dreamer's private universe, and is therefore incommunicable. Yet the dreaming power is closely connected with the creative faculties, which are powers of communication. This is the paradox that Bottom struggles with:

I have had a most rare vision. I have had a dream, past the wit of man to say what a dream it was: man is but an ass, if he go about to expound this dream. Methought I was—there is no man can tell what. Methought I was—and methought I had—but man is but a patched fool, if he will offer to say what methought I had. The eye of man hath not heard, the ear of man hath not seen, man's hand is not able to taste, his tongue to conceive, nor his heart to report, what my dream was. I will get Peter Quince to write a ballad of this dream: it shall be called Bottom's Dream, because it hath no bottom; and I will sing it in the latter end of a play, before the Duke: peradventure, to make it the more gracious, I shall sing it at her death.

Nobody knows what the last phrase means, but the scrambled metaphors do not quite conceal the biblical echo: "Eye hath not seen, nor ear heard, neither have entered into the heart of man, the things which God hath prepared." It would be wrong to sentimentalize Bottom, but equally wrong not to feel that perhaps Bottom, with what Puck calls his own fool's eyes, has seen something in the heart of comedy that our wisdom does not see, just as the insane Lear sees something in the heart of tragedy that our sanity does not see. It is quite consistent with the use of incredible events and the demand for an uncritical response in Shakespearean comedy that such oracular things should be said, or hinted at, by characters even simpler than we are.

There is a similar hint of folly sensing a kind of experience concealed to wisdom in Caliban's "isle is full of noises" speech. But the context of the romances is different, and this difference we have now to examine. The romances, in the first place, set up a hierarchy of behavior, more clearly stratified than we find in the comedies. We can see at least five levels of it in all the romances. On the highest level is the providential deity or its human counterpart Prospero; next come the hero and heroine; next the minor characters who represent a middle level of fidelity or common sense—Helicanus, Camillo, Pisanio, Gonzalo. Below these are, first, the clownish or absurd, and below that the evil or villainous. One represents primarily human nature without nurture, in Prospero's phrase; the other rationally corrupted nature, the evil that can result only from perverted intelligence. In *Pericles* the evil level is represented by Antiochus and his daughter who nearly kill Pericles, and by Cleon and Dionyza who nearly kill Marina. The nearest thing to a clown in *Pericles* is Boult, and

Boult, we notice, is redeemable in part: when we leave him he is even willing to face respectable women in order to help Marina. In the more somber *Cymbeline* there is no clown except Cloten, who is as evil as his stupidity will allow him to be, and though that comes far short of the cold malice of Iachimo, there is no place in the recognition scene for him. In *The Winter's Tale* we have clowns and rustics who become gentlemen, and very decent ones at that; and Autolycus, for all his talk about being committed to vice, eventually settles into the role of accepted clown, like Parolles at the end of *All's Well*. A lower depth of evil is reached by the jealous Leontes. In *The Tempest* villainy is represented by Sebastian and more particularly by Antonio; the clowns are Stephano and Trinculo, and Caliban is on their level. He is of course full of original sin, and he does not take the view of Prospero that Prospero clearly thinks ought to be taken of him, but his natural propensity to evil does not prevent him from still being likable and having his share of human dignity. Caliban, too, seems ready for some improvement at the end of the play.

We can generalize these levels by saying that in all the romances there is a tendency to set an idealized or noble situation over against an evil or demonic parody of it. We have noticed this construction in *Pericles* with the incestuous and idealized father-daughter unions, and it appears also in *Cymbeline*, where a union of Britain and Rome is set over against a nationalistic Britain represented by Cloten and the Queen, and an Italian Rome represented by Iachimo. In all the romances except *Pericles* (where the episodic structure is what prevents it), the really evil characters are suddenly and most unplausibly converted at the end, if they are still alive. This is partly because they are noblemen who have gone wrong, as Gilbert would say, and in fact as Shakespeare says of the bandits in *The Two Gentlemen of Verona*. Thus in the romances there is no *idiotes* figure except insofar as the villain has that role. The function of this *idiotes*-villain is to injure or delay or prevent the festive conclusion, and when the recognition is reached he disappears into it, his function performed. His forgiveness, again, is primarily structural, not moral: Shakespeare's emphasis on reconciliation is a technical emphasis rather than an oozing through of personal benevolence. Thus in the romances no one is left at the end to take the detached spectator's role. We are left with a sense of the action going on into a world where nobody is watching. That may be one reason for the curious device of summoning the cast for explanations afterward, though it is true that this is not confined to the romances. But the romances seem to point to some postdramatic world where the questions of illusion and of a detached or alienated spectator are no longer raised.

An emphasis on theatrical illusion is a mark of sophistication, and Shakespeare's sophisticated comedies are early ones. In *Love's Labour's Lost* certain theatrical conventions, such as concealment, are used so extravagantly that they parody the conventions. The characters make several references to being in a play, which is another sign of sophistication. Such comedy does not hold a mirror up to nature, but it frequently holds a mirror up to another mirror, and brings its resolution out of a double illusion. Petruchio does not argue Katharina out of her shrewishness: he simply shows her the reflection of her shrewishness in himself. But there is still an element of deliberate illusion in the stylized, almost ballet-like action of the play, which is emphasized by being set over against the illusory world created around Sly. The much simpler scheme of an ideal world parodied by a demonic one, which we find in the romances, is a part of their primitiveness.

We have noticed the archaic features in the romances. The narrator of *Pericles* is the antique Gower; the "peripety" of *Cymbeline* is a vision of ghosts chanting verse as crude as Chaucer's rhyme of Sir Thopas; *The Winter's Tale* keeps insisting on how like its story is to an "old tale," its closest literary relatives the ballads sold by Autolycus. The crisis of this last play is the revival of Hermione, who begins to speak as soon as Paulina pronounces the magic words "Our Perdita is found," and thus announces the fulfilling of Apollo's oracle. It is impossible that Hermione can really have come to life, and we can believe other explanations if we like, though they involve equally great strains on credulity. For instance, would Leontes really have regarded Paulina with such reverence if she had been keeping the live Hermione concealed from him all this time? Ovid tells us that Pygmalion did not dare ask Venus that his statue should come alive, but only that he might have a girl "like" his statue. Venus, however, who, being a goddess, spoke only the language of myth, metaphor, and metamorphosis, ignored this and brought his statue to life. Shakespeare is clearly of Venus' mind in such matters. Yet it is equally difficult to believe that the new Hermione had her origin in Giulio Romano's chisel instead of in the old Hermione, and perhaps we had better stop trying to believe things and simply look at what is in front of us, which is a dramatic exhibition of death and revival. And it seems clear that we shall get further with that if our attitude is more like that of Bottom commenting on his dream than of Jaques commenting on the human capacity for illusion.

The Winter's Tale is a diptych, in which the first part is the "winter's tale" proper, the story of the jealousy of Leontes, the slandering of Hermione, and the perilous exposure of Perdita. The second part, the last two acts, is the story of Florizel's love, Perdita's recognition, and the revival of Hermione. Shakespeare's main source, Greene's *Pandosto*, is almost entirely confined to the first part; for the rest Shakespeare appears to be on his own. There are parallels and contrasts in the construction: the contrast in imagery, the first part full of winter and storm and chaos and the second all spring and revival and fertility, is not easily missed. The first part begins with Archidamas speaking of how the old people in Sicilia would wish to live until the king had a son, and proceeds to the court of Sicilia, where an attempt is made to delay a return to Bohemia. Then Leontes becomes a jealous *senex*, after which Camillo flees to Bohemia. The second part begins with Time telling us that a generation has passed, proceeds to the court of Bohemia and an attempt to delay a return to Sicilia, and exhibits Polixenes in the role of a jealous and suspicious *senex*, after which Camillo flees to Sicilia. In the first part Mamillius dies and Perdita is very near death; in the second part Florizel, who reminds Leontes of Mamillius and becomes his heir, marries Perdita, after (as Bottom says when he has died in the role of Pyramus and sprung up again) "the wall is down that parted their fathers."

The jealous Leontes is the *idiotes* of the play, the focus of the anticomic mood, and the first part of the action is the anticomedy that his jealousy constructs. We begin with references to an innocent childhood when Leontes and Polixenes were "twinned lambs," and then suddenly plunge from the reminiscence of this pastoral paradise into a world of superstition and obsession. Leontes has a great fear of becoming an object of ridicule or comic butt, though, as Antigonus mutters in an aside, that is precisely what he does become. The horror of the world he creates is expressed mainly in the imagery of sacrifice: he wants to gain rest by burning Hermione alive; his courtiers offer to be or provide sacrifices in her place, and eventually the sacrificial role settles on Mamillius. The first part ends in a storm which, like the storm in *Lear* (which it echoes in its bear and sea), is described in such a way as to suggest an unsettling of the order of nature. We are told later that "all the instruments which aided to expose the child were even then lost when it was found," as though a new generation had to grow up in the desert before the festival world could be reached. Some very curious echoes indicate the starting of a new action: part one ends with the clown hearing the cries of Antigonus as the bear tears out his shoulder bone; part two begins with the same clown hearing the cries of Autolycus pretending that his shoulder blade is out.

The normal action of a comedy moves from irrational law to festivity, which symbolizes a movement from one form of reality to another. The world of tyranny and irrational law is a world where what is real is given us arbitrarily as a datum, something we must accept or somehow come to terms with. This is a spectator's reality, the reality we see to be "out there." The world of the final festival is a world where reality is what is created by human desire, as the arts are created. There is something of this in *The Winter's Tale:* Leontes takes a morbid pleasure in facing what he thinks are facts, and insists on the tangible external reality of his world: "I do smell't and feel't," he says. The creative arts are also deeply involved in the recognition scene: painting, sculpture, poetry, and music are all introduced or referred to, and several conceptions of art, from the idealism of Polixenes and the realism of Romano to the nonsense of Autolycus' ballads, are mentioned.

But the action of *The Winter's Tale* is clearly something other than a movement from external to created reality. In the first place, the world of Leontes' jealousy does not exist at all: only the consequences of believing in it exist. In the second place, the power of human desire that revives Hermione and brings the lovers together is identical, first, with the power of nature to bring new life out of death, and second, with the will of Apollo, whose oracle is being fulfilled. The action, therefore, moves from appearance to reality, from mirage to substance. Once the real world is reached, the mirage becomes nothingness. The real world, however, has none of the customary qualities of reality. It is the world symbolized by nature's power of renewal; it is the world we want; it is the world we hope our gods would want for us if they were worth worshiping. But it is "monstrous to our human reason," according to Paulina, and its truth "is so like an old tale that the verity of it is in strong suspicion." Such things happen in stories, not in life, and the world *The Winter's Tale* leaves us with is neither an object of knowledge nor of belief.

It would be an object of belief, of course, or symbolize one, if we could feel that *The Winter's Tale* was an allegory. I have been assuming that it is not: that in Shakespeare the meaning of the play is the play, there being nothing to be abstracted from the total experience of the play. Progress in grasping the meaning is a progress, not in seeing more in the play, but in seeing more of it. Further progress takes us from the individual plays to the class of things called plays, to the "meaning" of drama as a whole. That meaning, again, is our total experience of drama. The center of that experience is the fact that drama is doing, through the identity of myth and metaphor, what its ritual predecessors tried to do by the identity of sympathetic magic: unite the human and the natural worlds. But the world where this unity can be achieved is clearly not the world of ordinary experience, in which man is an alienated spectator. The world we are looking at in the conclusion of *The Winter's Tale* is not an object of belief so much as an imaginative model of desire. The last words, "Hastily lead away," summon us like a beckoning to a new and impossible world, and our cue is to say, like Antipholus of Syracuse when confronted by a wife he never saw before: "I'll entertain the offered fallacy."

IV. *The Return from the Sea*

Comedy, like all forms of art that are presented in time, is primarily an impetus toward completing a certain kind of movement. We have been trying to characterize the nature of the comic drive, and have called it a drive toward identity. This is essentially a social identity, which emerges when the ascendant society of the early part of the play, with its irrational laws, lusts, and tyrannical whims, is dissolved and a new society crystallizes around the marriage of the central characters. It has also an individual form, an awakening to self-knowledge, which is typically a release from a humor or a mechanical form of repetitive behavior.

Shakespearean romantic comedy presents the full or completed form of this movement; ironic comedy presents incomplete or divergent forms of it. As a rule irony is intelligible only as a frustration of a completed movement which is presented in romance: thus we need to have the normal or romantic design at least unconsciously in our minds to understand the parodies of it that irony supplies. We may often think of the happy ending as perfunctory, and sometimes it may seem that, but even in the most sardonic comedies we should not assume that Shakespeare had a different kind of ending in mind that he could have provided for a more highbrow audience. The more highbrow audience might be more ironically minded, more bored with the conventional romantic ending, more inclined to be flattered at being asked to settle for some new variant of it. But Shakespeare, like Shylock, insists on carrying out his contract to the letter. His festive conclusions with their multiple marriages are not concessions: they are conventions built into the structure of the play from the beginning.

The mythical or primitive basis of comedy is a movement toward the rebirth and renewal of the powers of nature, this aspect of literary comedy being expressed in the imagery more directly than in the structure. The mythical backbone of all literature is the cycle of nature, which rolls from birth to death and back again to rebirth. The first half of this cycle, the movement from birth to death, spring to winter, dawn to dark, is the basis of the great alliance of nature and reason, the sense of nature as a rational order in which all movement is toward the increasingly predictable. Such a conception of nature was of course deeply rooted in the Elizabethan mind: it extends even to the tendency to call anything natural that the writer is accustomed to, as when Sidney expresses horror at the custom of wearing rings in the nose instead of in "the fit and natural places of the ears." In drama, tragedy, the history play (always very close to tragedy) and pure irony (*e.g. Troilus and Cressida*) are centered on this first half. There may be many surprises in the last act of a Shakespearean tragedy, but the pervading feeling is of something inevitable working itself out. The histories deal similarly with a kind of "karma" or continuous force of evil action which produces its own inevitable consequences. In the *Henry VI* plays the original sin of the House of Lancaster in deposing Richard and pushing Edmund Mortimer out of the way releases a flood of such "karma" which isolates and overwhelms Talbot in Part One, Duke Humphrey in Part Two, and the gentle and ineffectual Henry VI himself in Part Three. The organizing conception of the history play is the wheel of fortune, which, according to Chaucer's monk, started turning with the fall of Lucifer, and is repeated in the fall of every great man, who discovers with Wolsey that

> When he falls, he falls like Lucifer,
> Never to hope again.

The wheel of fortune is a tragic conception: it is never genuinely a comic one, though a history play may achieve a technically comic conclusion by stopping the wheel turning halfway. Thus *Henry V* ends with triumphant conquest and a royal marriage, though, as the epilogue reminds us, King Henry died almost immediately and sixty years of unbroken disaster followed. In *Henry VIII* there are three great falls, those of Buckingham, Wolsey, and Queen Catherine, and three corresponding rises, those of Cromwell, Cranmer, and Anne Boleyn. The play ends with the triumph of the last three, leaving the audience to remember that the wheel went on turning and brought them down too. Being a strong king, Henry VIII turns the wheel himself, and is not turned by it, like Richard II, but history never can end as a comedy does, except for the polite fiction, found in Cranmer's prophecy at the end of the play, that the reigning monarch is a Messianic ruler.

Comedy, however, is based on the second half of the great cycle, moving from death to rebirth, decadence to renewal, winter to spring, darkness to a new dawn. We notice that three comedies, *The Winter's Tale, Twelfth Night*, and *A Midsummer Night's Dream*, have solstitial titles: perhaps it is *The Winter's Tale* that expresses the cyclical imagery of comedy most clearly. The "winter's tale," properly speaking, begins with Leontes' guards coming to seize Hermione at the moment when Mamillius is about to whisper his tale into his mother's ear, and it ends in a tremendous storm in which Antigonus perishes and the infant Perdita is exposed. Sixteen years pass, and a new dramatic action begins with a new generation, an action of irresistibly pushing life, heralded by Autolycus' song of the daffodils, and growing to a climax in the great sheepshearing festival scene, where the power of life in nature over the whole year is symbolized by a dance of twelve satyrs. The reviving force pushes on, brings Florizel and Perdita together despite the most frantic parental opposition, discloses the secret of Perdita's birth, brings Hermione to life from a statue, and finally renews life in Leontes.

The same symbolism is presented negatively in *Love's Labour's Lost*, where the audience is cheated of the comic conclusion. The courtiers present themselves to their ladies, first as Russians (Russia to an Elizabethan audience meant primarily cold winters), then as themselves. But the four Jacks panting for their Jills are disappointed; the ladies go away, and the breakup of the comic mood is symbolized by the two lovely songs of spring and winter, in which winter has the last word. Similar imagery comes occasionally into many comedies, as in this oracular speech of Helena in *All's Well*:

> But with the word the time will bring on summer,
> When briars shall have leaves as well as thorns,
> And be as sweet as sharp. We must away;
> Our waggon is prepared, and time revives us.
> All's well that ends well: still the fine's the crown.

This movement from sterility to renewed life is as natural as the tragic movement, because it happens. But though natural it is somehow irrational: the sense of the alliance of nature with reason and predictable order is no longer present. We can see that death is the inevitable result of birth, but new life is not the inevitable result of death. It is hoped for, even expected, but at its core is something unpredictable and mysterious, something that belongs to the imaginative equivalents of faith, hope, and love, not to the rational virtues. The conception of the *same* form of life passing through death to rebirth of course goes outside the order of nature altogether. Yet this conception is so central in Shakespearean romance, as Thaisa revives from a "block" and Hermione from a statue, that perhaps what really emerges in the recognition scenes of these romances is the primitive feeling, which is incorporated in Christianity, that it is *death* that is somehow unnatural, even though it always happens.

We live in an ironic age, and we tend to think, in Freudian terms, of "wish fulfillment" as confined to dreams, a helpless and shadowy counterpart of a "reality principle." In watching tragedy we are impressed by the reality of the illusion: we feel that, for instance, the blinding of Gloucester, though not really happening, is the kind of thing that can and does happen. In watching romantic comedy we are impressed by the illusion of the reality: we feel that, for instance, the conversion of Oliver and Duke Frederick at the end of *As You Like It* is the kind of thing that can't happen, yet we see it happening. In the action of a Shakespearean comedy, however, the kind of force associated with "wish fulfillment" is not helpless or purely a matter of dreams. It is, in the first place, a power as deeply rooted in nature and reality as its opponent; in the second place, it is a power that we see, as the comedy proceeds, taking over and informing the predictable world.

Yet there is a residually irrational element in such comedy, which expresses itself in a great variety of unlikely incidents: unexpected turns in the plot, gratuitous coincidences, unforeseen changes of heart in certain characters, arbitrary interference with the action by fairies or gods or characters who do not enter the play at all. We have already seen how Shakespeare deliberately chooses incredible plots and emphasizes the unlikelihood of his conclusions. The drive toward a comic conclusion is so powerful that it breaks all the chains of probability in the plot, of habit in the characters, even of expectation in the audience; and what emerges at the end is not a logical consequence of the preceding action, as in tragedy, but something more like a metamorphosis.

I have spoken of the readiness with which dramatic assumptions can be translated into propositions or axioms of belief. Tragic assumptions usually turn out to be propositions about a metaphysical fate or about the moral fatality of characteristic acts. The sense of fatality can seldom be far away from tragedy and is usually expressed there, as it is when Romeo speaks of "inauspicious stars," or Gloucester of the indifference and carelessness of the gods. In the nineteenth century it was fashionable to quote such passages to show that Shakespeare was a nineteenth-century pessimist. Those who wished to save him for free will and moral responsibility, on the other hand, could point to the fact that fatality usually cooperates with character: the witches in *Macbeth* may be, as Holinshed says, goddesses of destiny, but it is clear that Macbeth has made a subconscious pact with them before the play begins. In comedy, where there is a sense of violent manipulation of plot, of characters leaping into new roles, or events driving toward a renewing transformation in the teeth of all probability, it is easy to arrive at moral axioms about a divine providence.

Thus in Gascoigne's *Supposes*, which has a plot that seems to have suggested some features of *The Taming of the Shrew*, one of the characters turns out to be, according to a frequent New Comedy device, the son of another character, stolen from him in infancy. This provokes the reflection from the father: "And you, Philogano, may think that God in heaven above ordained your coming hither at this present, to the end I might recover my lost son whom by no other means I could ever have found out." The remark inspires an equally sententious rejoinder: "Surely, sir, I think no less, for I think that not so much as a leaf falleth from the tree without the ordinance of God." In Machiavelli's *Mandragola* we get pious reflections of a morally different but structurally identical kind. In this play the main theme is the attempt of a young man to get into the bed of a faithful and virtuous married woman. He bamboozles her husband, talks over her mother, and bribes a venal priest, whereupon the heroine reflects that she may as well acquiesce in the goings-on and get what enjoyment from them she can, as the coincidence of having a foolish husband, an unscrupulous mother, and a scoundrelly confessor has persuaded her that the affair must be the will of God.

Shakespeare does not use God to underwrite his comic plots in quite this way, but the conclusion is frequently ascribed to characters or powers who act as though they were agents of providence. In three of the romances a deity, Diana in *Pericles*, Jupiter in *Cymbeline*, and a hidden and off-stage Apollo in *The Winter's Tale*, brings about or is involved in the conclusion. Where it is accomplished by a human being, as it is in *The Tempest* and *Measure for Measure*, that character has about him something of the mysterious aura of divinity, symbolized by magic or sanctity. We are not surprised that Prospero is a magician, or to find the Duke in *Measure for Measure* disguised as a saintly friar, eventually marrying a girl who intended to be a nun. The themes of magic and sanctity appear vestigially in *As You Like It*, where a saintly hermit converts Duke Frederick and Rosalind pretends that she has a magician uncle who will provide some of the metamorphosis at the end. Portia, too, pretends to retire to a convent, and seems to have some magical or sibylline knowledge of a "letter" about Antonio's mercantile ventures, though she is not going to tell Antonio (or us) how she came by the knowledge. In *Much Ado* there is a kind of parody of a modern detective story when Dogberry and his group, by their sheer consistency in blundering, help to force the story of Claudio and Hero into a comedy of renewal. As Borachio says: "What your wisdoms could not discover, these shallow fools have brought to light," reminding us of the scriptural passage about God using the foolish things of the world to confound the wise.

We have noticed how frequently the comic action begins by setting up a harsh or irrational law, two typical examples being in *A Comedy of Errors* and *A Midsummer Night's Dream*. In both these instances, the law is proclaimed by a duke who announces that it is completely unbreakable and that his integrity as a ruler is bound up with enforcing it. The affinity with the common folklore theme of a king's rash promise becoming a binding oath is strongly marked. In both instances the law disappears as soon as the action circumvents it. At the beginning of *A Comedy of Errors* the Duke reiterates that the law prevents him from pardoning Aegeon without a bag of gold as ransom, but when at the end he is offered the gold he merely says: "It shall not need: thy father hath his life." Theseus similarly, after telling Hermia that he administers a law "which by no means we may extenuate," abandons the law in the fourth act and says to her father "I will overbear your will." The Duke of Venice also discovers a good many extra powers of discretion as soon as the quibble about blood is pointed out to him.

Thus the irrational law represents the comic equivalent of a social contract, something we must enter into if the final society is to take shape. The irrational law, also, belongs to that aspect of nature which appears, in other contexts, rational, centered in the inevitable movement from birth to death. As the end of the comic action usually reconciles and incorporates its predecessor, what corresponds to the irrational law has been internalized, transformed to an inner source of coherence. The fact that Solinus and Theseus veto the law by their own will would mean in life that we were regressing from the rule of law to a personal whim, but in the action of comedy it means precisely the opposite. The dukes of Ephesus and Venice merely ratify the fact that Aegeon and Antonio have been redeemed by a higher power than money. Athens was wrong in its method of imposing true love, but it remains true that in romance the only tolerable possibilities for a heroine are true love, chastity, and death. And even as regards the Athenian law Hermia says, with the whole wisdom of Thalia behind her:

> it is a customary cross,
> As due to love as thoughts and dreams and sighs.

The internalizing movement of law is clearest in *Measure for Measure*, where the Duke leaves Vienna to return and be invisibly present in his society. His return at the end to preside over the *cognitio* indicates that the movement has been completed. Dogberry and Shallow, too, however ridiculous in themselves, somehow manage to suggest a permanent social order that is less so.

In a typically festive conclusion all previous conflicts are forgiven and forgotten. In ordinary life this phrase is seldom a moral reality, because it is usually a contradiction: to forgive an offense implies that the offense was real; to forget it implies that something in it was not, and forgetting is not a voluntary act as forgiveness is. To forget implies a break in the continuity of memory, a kind of amnesia in which the previous action is put out of our reach. Normally, we can forget in this way only when we wake up from a dream, when we pass from one world into another, and we often have to think of the main action of a comedy as "the mistakes of a night," as taking place in a dream or nightmare world that the final scene suddenly removes us from and thereby makes illusory.

The Book of Job is technically a comedy by virtue of its final chapter, which tells us that God restored to Job everything he had lost with interest, including three very beautiful daughters named Jemima, Keziah, and Keren-happuch. We stop and say to ourselves: Job had lost three daughters, and is it really true that a man who has lost three daughters could be completely consoled with three brand-new daughters, however beautiful or impressively named? Would he not still feel that he had suffered an irreparable loss? For the suggestion is that this renewal annihilates the sense of loss itself, which the renewals of ordinary life, such as second marriages, are not intended to do. As Pericles says to the gods: "Your present kindness/Makes my past miseries sports." The author of Job has solved the moral problem of his play in the usual comic fashion, by cutting its Gordian knot. But we can accept this solution only by thinking of the world of Job's reward as a different world from the nightmare world of misery and boils and uncomprehending comforters.

The sense of waking up from a dream is frequent in Shakespeare too, most explicitly, of course, in the play which is explicitly called a dream. If we are to accept the reconciliation of Claudio and Hero, of Angelo and Mariana, of Imogen and Posthumus, we have to think of them also as awakenings, where it is possible to forget as well as forgive what has happened. Yet the play would be pointless if there were not some reality in the previous tragic complications with which the final scene is still continuous. Renewal, the *telos* or final cause of comedy, is in some way both return and the opposite of return. In ordinary life we are conscious only of the discontinuity between dream and waking. In drama this is not the whole story. A tragedy employs omens and oracles and ghosts and other anticipators of the final catastrophe to emphasize the connection between the two worlds. In comedy there is a conclusion of awakening which incorporates the dream action, like Adam's awakening to find his dream

true in *Paradise Lost*, which Keats saw as a central symbol of
the imagination. We awake in a world possessed and informed by something in the dream, or, as Hippolyta says:

> But all the story of the night told over,
> And all their minds transfigured so together,
> More witnesseth than fancy's images,
> And grows to something of great constancy;
> But, howsoever, strange and admirable.

The festive ending of a comedy represents what the audience normally regards as on the whole a desirable solution to
its action. This means that the action itself contains features
that are undesirable: the ascendancy of a cruel tyrant or a
foolish rival, the separation or estrangement of lovers, and
the like. Such things are undesirable from the point of view
of a standard that we have, at least potentially, in our minds
before the play begins. The conclusion restores that anteced-
ent sense of the desirable; but it does not simply reproduce
it, because we do not know what it is before we start fashioning it against the action. It is the purpose of the action to
define and clarify something new which is also the old re-
formed or metamorphosed.

It is possible, of course, to bring into the theater with us a
more or less definite notion of what is desirable and demand
that the action lead simply to reproducing it. This demand is
the core of the conception in the arts that we call the sentimental, the movement that leads back, not to the beginning
of the action of the play, but to a state of our minds before
the play which remains unchanged by its action. Synge's

Playboy of the Western World caused riots on its first performance partly because its audience could not make its conclusion incorporate what they had already decided was the
desirable picture of rural Irish life, an Arcadia full of
toilworn Mother Machrees and twinkling-eyed Father
O'Flynns. The sentimental is closely linked with the desire to
renounce adult experience and return to the protected and
secure world of childhood. Its typically literary expression is a
letter to the *New York Times Book Review* asking for more
information about a poem beginning "Now I lay me down to
sleep." One moment in British drama that most of us would
agree to be sentimental is the moment in Barrie's *Peter Pan*
in which a character turns to the audience and begs them to
believe in fairies, or at least to say that they do, which for
sentimentality is much the same thing. There is a famous
story about the reaction of a Victorian lady to *Antony and
Cleopatra:* "How different from the domestic relations in
our own royal family!" The basis of this remark is the mental
attitude of the audience appealed to by the sentimental domestic comedy of the eighteenth and nineteenth centuries.

The sentimental is usually regarded as culturally substand-
ard, because it denies the forward movement in art, the sense
of fresh discovery in every renewal of familiar values. What
it appeals to is stock response, a set of associations that one
already has or at least knows about. Things that demand
loyalty, such as the symbols of church and state, operate by
simple continuity or repetition of the familiar: the same
creed recited every Sunday, the same flag saluted in school

every morning. This is why religious or patriotic art is usually sentimental in expression. Sentimentality is instinctively tearful, even at weddings, partly because it resists, as a child would do, the inexorable advance of all experience in time, which it tries to arrest by nostalgia. In trying to distinguish structure from mood, I said that while structure was the focus of a community, uniformity of mood, which demands uniformity of response, breaks down the community into a mob: the kind of audience appealed to by farce, Grand Guignol melodrama, and extreme didacticism. Sentimentality is the subjective equivalent of the mob's stock response to mood. The sentimental is withdrawn but not detached; it is an egocentric feeling but not an individualized one; it is gregarious but not social.

I have spent some time on the conception of the sentimental because a quality very like it, yet very different, is central to Shakespeare's comedy. The sentimental is a fixation on the familiar, and so leads us back toward our subjective childhood. But there is another kind of vision in the arts, represented by Blake's *Songs of Innocence* and Virgil's Fourth Eclogue, where the return is not to childhood but to a state of innocence symbolized by childhood, the state recalled in the stories of the Garden of Eden, of the Golden Age, and of the myriad stories that derive from them, in the pastoral convention and elsewhere. This vision, though often presented as a historical event in the past and as deeply traditional, avoids the subjective pull of the sentimental, because it is a vision of something never seen or experienced, and hence, when it is presented as something we return to, it is a genuinely new vision. This is closer to the kind of vision that Shakespeare's comedies and romances, which are never sentimental although they constantly employ what seems like the same kind of material, are based on.

The action of a Shakespearean comedy, then, is not simply cyclical but dialectical as well: the renewing power of the final action lifts us into a higher world, and separates that world from the world of the comic action itself. This dialectical element in Shakespeare's comic structure we have now to examine. The first feature of it is the parallel between the structure of a romantic comedy and the central myth of Christianity: the parallel that made Dante call his poem a *commedia*. The framework of the Christian myth is the comic framework of the Bible, where man loses a peaceable kingdom, staggers through the long nightmare of tyranny and injustice which is human history, and eventually regains his original vision. Within this myth is the corresponding comedy of the Christian life. We first encounter the law in its harsh tyrannical form of an external barrier to action, a series of negative commands, and we are eventually set free of this law, not by breaking it, but by internalizing it: it becomes an inner condition of behavior, not an external antagonist as it is to the criminal.

Two of Shakespeare's comedies present the action within this familiar Christian setting. In *The Merchant of Venice* the supporter of the irrational law is a Jew, or at least what Shakespeare's audience assumed to be a Jew. Shylock is frequently called a devil, because his role at the trial is the diabolical one of an accuser who demands death. When he says: "My deeds upon my head!" and prefers the seed of Barabbas to Christians, he is echoing the Jews at the trial of Christ. The redeeming power which baffles him is the blood that he cannot have. His insistence on his bond and on justice is countered by Portia's explicitly Christian appeal to mercy, and his claim to his bond is not denied until he has renounced mercy. In the background of the imagery are allusions to the story of the prodigal son, the parable which sums up, in epitome, the whole Christian story of the exile and return of man to his home.

Measure for Measure, as its title indicates, is also based on the theme of the moral bankruptcy of law. The play turns on the hairline contrast between the situation of Claudio and of Angelo, the second not being revealed to us until the first has reached its climax, in Claudio's prison cell. Claudio is betrothed and anticipates his conjugal rights; Angelo is betrothed and deserts Mariana because the financial arrangements fall through. Legally, this makes Claudio a condemned criminal and leaves Angelo a model of virtue. In the area of equity, or the personal considerations of justice, it makes the impetuous Claudio likable and the cautious Angelo a most unattractive cold fish. The knowledge of good and evil clearly does not lead to any real knowledge of either good or evil. It is explicitly said that Angelo's right to enforce the law depends on his own immunity from temptation. In the ordinary social terms that a problem comedy might be thought to deal with, such a statement is preposterous: law, whatever may be said for or against it, certainly does not depend for its validity on the private morality of the judge who administers it. But in the terms of reference employed by *Measure for Measure* the statement is crucial, and quite consistent. If it were possible for one man to observe the law in a state of perfect innocence, the whole foolish experiment of leaving Angelo in charge of society would be justified, and there would be no hope that the Duke could ever return in any other shape than that of a helpless confessor of victims.

The enormous disproportion between grace and merit, which has already met us several times, recurs all through Shakespearean comedy, where "grace" is a centrally important thematic word. In *Love's Labour's Lost* this theme is given us in the language of Courtly Love, which used the language of religion in its own context. Berowne protests against the academic retreat by saying:

> For every man with his affects is born,
> Not by might mastered, but by special grace.

There are several suggestions that the King of Navarre's "curious-knotted garden" is a delusive Eden in which the real knowledge sought is "the thing I am forbid to know." The theme of salvation by one's own merit is picked up by the Princess when she speaks of it as a "heresy" "fit for these days," and when she remarks: "All pride is willing pride." Berowne finally confesses that the surrender of the courtiers to the demands of love is a falsehood that "purifies itself and turns to grace," but Rosaline tells him that he must first undergo a "reformation" in which he has to suppress his uncharitable spirit of mockery:

> Whose influence is begot of that loose grace
> Which shallow laughing hearers give to fools.

In Shakespeare, as in all his contemporaries, the ordinary cycle of nature that rolls from spring to winter to spring again is the middle of three modes of reality. It is the ordinary physical world that, according to the theologians, man entered with his fall. Above it is the nature that God intended man to live in, the home symbolized by the biblical Garden of Eden and the Classical legend of the Golden Age, a world of a perpetual fertility where it was spring and autumn at once. To this world, or to the inward equivalent of it, man strives to return through the instruments of law, religion, morality, and (much more important in Shakespeare's imagery) education and the arts. Thus it is said of Posthumus that he took so readily to his education that "in's spring became a harvest." All the arts are employed as regenerative symbols in the romances, but the most important one by far is the traditional one, music. Music is traditional because all that is now left of this upper world of nature is the ordered revolution of the starry spheres, with their inaudible music that symbolizes the harmony of the soul. This harmony of the soul, in its turn, is symbolized by female chastity, which in all pastoral romance down to Milton's *Comus* is an attribute of the higher order of nature, and a containing of spiritual energy. The central symbol of this upper world is the moon, the boundary between the two orders of nature and the habitation of Cynthia or Diana, the goddess of chastity.

Below the cycle of nature, or the ordinary physical world, is the abyss of disorder which Shakespeare often summons up by the word "nothing," and symbolizes, most frequently, by the tempest. It is also the world of the devouring time which sweeps everything into annihilation. The subjective equivalents for storm and tempest are madness, illusion, or death itself. As the comic action proceeds, the middle world of ordinary experience disappears into the world above it, and separates itself from the world below it. A Gentleman in *The Winter's Tale*, reporting the recognition scene of the finding of Perdita, says that the King and Camillo "looked as they had heard of a world ransomed, or one destroyed," and it is the separation between redemption and destruction which constitutes the dialectic of romantic comedy.

The images of chaos, tempest, illusion, madness, darkness, death, belong to the middle action of the comedy, in the phase of confused identity. It is at this point, the low point of the hero's or heroine's fortunes, as a rule, that the comic dialectic is formed. All the tempest comedies, *A Comedy of Errors, Twelfth Night, Pericles, The Tempest* itself, prominently display the imagery of madness: almost everybody in *Twelfth Night* is said at some time or other to be mad, and this theme comes to its climax in the practical joke played on Malvolio, where Malvolio's noble thoughts of the soul are a pretext for keeping him shut up. A similar theme appears in the equally unpleasant scene in *The Taming of the Shrew* where Petruchio compels Katharina to deny the evidence of her senses. Olivia says of Malvolio: "Why, this is very midsummer madness," and perhaps this very common phrase accounts for the title of *A Midsummer Night's Dream*, the action of which appears to take place nearer the first of May. A similar repetition of the theme of madness looms conspicuously in *A Comedy of Errors*, which introduces a rudimentary psychiatrist to exorcise it.

In *A Comedy of Errors* and *The Merchant of Venice* the action passes through a threat of death to the central character. In *Measure for Measure* the confrontation with death is symmetrical and thoroughgoing, with the disguised Duke in a curiously macabre psychopomp role. Every major male character in the play is threatened with death, though no one actually gets hurt much, except that a character who does not enter the play at all, the pirate Ragozine, expires of natural causes. In other plays, as previously remarked, it is the heroine who is threatened with death or who actually dies, as far as the imagery of the play is concerned. The convention of striking or wounding the heroine, much favored by Beaumont and Fletcher, appears in *Cymbeline* when Posthumus strikes the disguised Imogen, in *Pericles* when Marina is pushed back, or whatever the right stage direction is, and vestigially in *The Winter's Tale*, when Polixenes threatens to mutilate the beauty of Perdita. In the romances the confrontation with death is central to the action: the focus of it in *Pericles* is the attempt to murder Marina and in *Cymbeline* it is the prison in which Posthumus awaits death while experiencing the vision of his ultimate deliverance. Both here and in *The Winter's Tale* there seems, as in *Measure for Measure*, to be a deliberate effort to threaten as many and actually harm as few characters as possible, and in *The Tempest*, besides the plots to murder Alonso and Prospero, the Court Party is led into ordeals of madness and illusion which bring them to the verge of suicide. We may note the similarity to the convention of the detective story, where suspicion of a capital crime passes over all the main characters before it settles on one. It looks as though the "all's well that ends well" formula is deeply involved with a structure in which redemption from death, or even revival from death, is a central element.

As comedy normally works toward a reversal of its original postulates, the comic action is most simply described as a turning around. Hence Feste's reference to the whirligig of time in *Twelfth Night;* hence the byplay about the proverb "He that is giddy thinks the world turns round" at the end of *The Taming of the Shrew;* hence Benedick's final remark in *Much Ado:* "Man is a giddy thing, and this is my conclusion." But Benedick's word "giddy" echoes an earlier passage in the play, a vaporing speech of the drunken Borachio which appears to have no meaning and no relevance to anything, and which therefore ought to be looked at sharply:

Seest thou not, I say, what a deformed thief this fashion is? how giddily a turns about all the hot bloods between fourteen and five-and-thirty? sometime fashioning them like Pharaoh's soldiers in the reechy painting; sometime like god Bel's priests in the old church-window; sometime like the shaven Hercules in the smirched wormeaten tapestry, where his cod-piece seems as massy as his club?

Leaving aside the reference to primitive art, we notice that the word "fashion" is used in two senses. One sense is fashion as constant change, the principle of giddiness in life which enables people to take up and discard their moods, their attitudes, their prejudices, and their affections, and which diffuses through life that continuous amnesia of which comedy makes so distinctive a use. This fashion has a demonic side, which is why it is described as a deformed thief (the word deformed being called to our attention as a multiple pun). The other meaning is fashion in the sense of shaping or creating. What it shapes, in this speech of Borachio, is what we should now call personae, the dramatic attitudes people assume in society, and which makes life theatrical even as it makes the theater lifelike. But the conception of fashion as a shaping power has further overtones. The real turning around, in the comic action, is the reversal of the poet's presentation into the spectator's perception, and this reversal is completed when the comic action defines the world of its conclusion, and separates itself from the world of confusion and chaos below it.

There is a group of comedies, including *The Two Gentle-*

men of Verona, *As You Like It*, and *A Midsummer Night's Dream*, in which the action moves from a world of parental tyranny and irrational law into a forest. There the comic resolution is attained, and the cast returns with it into their former world. The forest world presents a society in contrast to the one outside it, as the court of Duke Senior is in contrast to the court of Duke Frederick. The forest society is more flexible and tolerant than its counterpart: the brigands in *The Two Gentlemen* are noblemen who have been banished for murders and "such like petty crimes" (their own phrase: we occasionally wonder whether, as in *Love's Labour's Lost*, the audience was not expected to take some of this play as deliberate hokum). It is associated with the "golden world" in *As You Like It* and with Robin Hood in both *As You Like It* and *The Two Gentlemen*. It is explicitly a dream world in *A Midsummer Night's Dream*, and at least a magical one in *As You Like It*, as its effect on Oliver and Duke Frederick indicates. This forest world I have elsewhere called the green world (from Keats' *Endymion*, 1.16), and it represents a structural principle found in various forms in all the comedies. It is the place where the upper or purely human world toward which the comic action moves begins to take shape, and around which that world crystallizes.

In *A Midsummer Night's Dream* the forest is inhabited by fairies. These fairies are spirits of the elements, and as such they are part of the cyclical processes of nature: when Oberon and Titania quarrel their dissensions are reflected in bad weather. In this play they appear to be autonomous, but it is clear that they are essentially related to human life, and this relation turns out to be one of service, ranging from the blessing of the house at the end to Peaseblossom's scratching Bottom's head. Properly employed, they are spirits of energy, who pinch the lazy maids, and of chastity, which, in Shakespearean romance as in *Comus*, is an attribute of the higher human world that separates itself from nonbeing. (In Milton the forest is sinister, but the reversal of the image does not alter the fact that the theme is also Shakespeare's theme.) Fairies reappear in *The Merry Wives*, which is linked to the forest comedies by virtue of the final scene, and here again they are agents of chastity. It is interesting that as such they are enemies of Falstaff's lustful desires, and yet Falstaff's realization that his tormentors are not fairies rings with an authentic disappointment:

And these are not fairies? I was three or four times in the thought they were not fairies; and yet the guiltiness of my mind, the sudden surprise of my powers, drove the grossness of the foppery into a received belief, in despite of the teeth of all rhyme and reason, that they were fairies. See now how wit may be made a Jack-a-Lent, when 'tis upon ill employment!

The forest or green world, then, is a symbol of natural society, the word natural here referring to the original human society which is the proper home of man, not the physical world he now lives in but the "golden world" he is trying to regain. This natural society is associated with things which in the context of the ordinary world seem unnatural, but which are in fact attributes of nature as a miraculous and irresistible reviving power. These associations include dream, magic and chastity or spiritual energy as well as fertility and renewed natural energies. Magic in Shakespeare's day was an "art," and we have seen that the arts, especially music, are also attributes of a world which, being natural for man, is a world in which art and nature are at one.

The Merchant of Venice has no forest, forests being difficult to accommodate to a Venetian setting, but Portia's house in Belmont is a place of magic, chastity, and mysterious music. In this play the dialectic of the two societies is worked out in an extremely elaborate imagery of worth and value. At one pole is the gold and wealth of Shylock, acquired by usury, including a ring worth a wilderness of monkeys, and in which his daughter ranks as one more possession. The other pole is represented by the father of Portia, who associates *his* daughter with three caskets of which the leaden one is the only one of value. Bassanio's ordeal is compared to the Argonautic voyage for the Golden Fleece, and in the background is an intricate verbal texture woven of the relation between reality and appearance and the relation between gain and hazard. A good deal of byplay about the value of rings comes into the final act, and the mercantile ventures of Antonio move from disaster to profit as soon as the comic action is completed.

In the romances there is a conflict between a society which is artificial in the modern sense, a courtly aristocracy full of all-too-human pride, passion, and selfishness, and another society which we may call a "natural society," in the paradoxical sense just established. This natural society develops from the green world of the forest comedies, and is associated with a figure who is either a healer or in some other way a preserver of life. In *Pericles* it is represented by Cerimon, a folklore doctor whose magical and musical skill not only revives Thaisa but has brought a whole society to life. As an admirer says:

> hundreds call themselves
> Your creatures, who by you have been restored.

In *Cymbeline* the focus of the natural society is Belarius, the foster father who brings up Cymbeline's sons in simple and primitive surroundings. In the plays used as sources by Shakespeare the character corresponding to Belarius is a magician, and in *Cymbeline* mysterious music proceeds from Belarius' cave. The preserver of Imogen's life is Pisanio, who brings her to Belarius' world and thus completes the movement of the flight of Cymbeline's children from calumny. Pisanio also has an association by proxy with the medical profession in the drug he gives to Imogen.

In *The Winter's Tale* the natural society is the rural society of Bohemia, at the center of which is the shepherd who is Perdita's foster father, and who preserved her at birth. No mysterious music is heard in this world except the ballads of Autolycus, though Autolycus complacently notes the Orpheus-like influence of his songs, "which so drew the rest of the herd to me that all their other senses stuck in ears." But it is music that awakens Hermione in another area of the natural society, the chapel of Paulina, where Hermione has apparently been preserved for years while dead to the court. We notice that the natural society is particularly the world in which the heroine—Thaisa, Fidele, Hermione—dies and comes back to life. In the same play, when the clown and shepherd protest to Autolycus that they are plain fellows and Autolycus replies "A lie; you are rough and hairy," there is a curious association in the background between the natural society of the play and the biblical Esau, sent to wander in the desert although the rightful heir. A similar Esau-Jacob echo comes into the interview between Lancelot Gobbo and his blind father when Gobbo is about to forsake a descendant of Jacob.

In *The Tempest* the whole action takes place in the natural society of the island, under the magic and music of Prospero. The connecting link with the Court Party is Gonzalo, who had the role of preserver of the infant Miranda's life before the action of the play begins, and whose response to the island is a reverie of a simple golden age of primitive equality and leisure. In the earlier *All's Well* the natural society is contained in Helena's magical power of healing the diseased king, but the speech of Lavache the clown, quoted in the previous essay, declaring his preference for "the house with the narrow gate," indicates that he too belongs to it. *Measure for Measure* seems to have no area of natural society beyond the moated grange in which the forsaken Mariana sits all day and sings of "lights that do mislead the morn."

The natural society is often simple and primitive, and so socially inferior to the court. The situation of *All's Well* turns on the social inferiority of Helena to Bertram, and the relation of Imogen to Posthumus is similar, or felt to be so by Cymbeline. Social promotion is rare, and we notice a curious snobbery in the romances that sometimes seems almost perverse. In *The Tempest* the cold-blooded Antonio is treated with considerably more respect than the amusing rascals Stephano and Trinculo; Perdita, obviously the person who ought to marry Florizel, can outwit Polixenes only by the fact that she is a real princess; Guiderius in *Cymbeline*, despite his great services to his country, must die for killing Cloten, and is only saved by the fact that he is a real prince. "The comedies of Shakespeare," wrote Walt Whitman, "are altogether unacceptable to America and democracy." It seems to me, on the other hand, that a democracy is in an even better position than Shakespeare's society to understand that princes and princesses may be wish-fulfillment dreams as well as social facts. It would hardly be possible to depict the absorbing and informing of a courtly society by what we have called a natural society without making the social symbols of the latter identical with those of the former.

I have spoken of the way in which drama begins with the renunciation of magic, when ritual acts designed to operate on the order of nature are enclosed by a myth. I said that when drama renounces magic in this way it gets it back again through the nature of poetic imagery itself, which assimilates the natural to the human order by analogy and identity, simile and metaphor. The traditional symbol of this lost and regained magic in human art is Orpheus. Orpheus is often mentioned by name in crucial passages where he obviously belongs, as in Lorenzo's speech on harmony in *The Merchant of Venice*, but in a wider and more general sense Orpheus is the hero of all four romances, the musical, magical, and pastoral power that awakens Thaisa and Hermione, that draws Ferdinand toward Miranda, that signalizes the ritual death of Imogen and that gives strange dreams to Caliban. We have seen that the wheel of nature in Shakespearean comedy is far bigger in its scope than the wheel of fortune that organizes the histories. The high point of the wheel of fortune is symbolized by the weeded garden in *Richard II*, the work of art that requires constant judgment and vigilance. This figure reappears in Prospero's monologue to Miranda about his general incompetence in finding the right people to "trash for over-topping." Its low point is represented by usurpation, tyranny, war, the execution of the innocent, and the like. But the wheel of fortune turns all at once: there is no dialectic in the historical plays, no glimpse of a redeemed or recreated world. We notice that coronation scenes in the histories are frequently accompanied by the disgrace or repudiation of a scapegoat figure: we have Fastolfe at the coronation of Henry VI and Falstaff at that of his predecessor. Similarly the coronation of Anne Boleyn is accompanied by the disgrace of Queen Catherine, and we are not surprised to find that it is a song about Orpheus that is sung to her in the hour of her humiliation, a reminder of the greater cycle that she enters into in the vision at her death.

The author of the epistle to the reader in the *Troilus and Cressida* Quarto remarks that the comedies of Shakespeare are sprung from the sea of Venus. So they are, but the foam-born Aphrodite who presides over the end of comedy belongs in the shallower shores of a much deeper ocean. This is the sea of chaos itself, the abyss of nothingness symbolized in the Bible by the monster leviathan, the dragon of the deep that only God, in God's own time, can hook and bring to land. In his speech before the walls of Harfleur, Henry V threatens to let loose the chaos of a looting and raping soldiery on the town, and says:

> We may as bootless spend our vain command
> Upon th' enraged soldiers in their spoil
> As send precepts to the leviathan
> To come ashore.

In *The Two Gentlemen of Verona* Proteus says:

> For Orpheus' lute was strung with poets' sinews,
> Whose golden touch could soften steel and stones,
> Make tigers tame, and huge leviathans
> Forsake unsounded deeps to dance on sands.

The Two Gentlemen of Verona is Shakespeare's most perfunctory comedy, and the speaker, Proteus, is a rather poor creature. But even so the contrast between the scope of history and the scope of comedy is very clear.

In the Bible the leviathan is not simply a whale or sea monster: it is both the power of tyranny, identified with Nebuchadnezzar and the Pharaoh of Egypt, and the abyss of lost identity. For by the principles of metaphor a sea monster can be the sea, and the sea can be the flood of annihilation that drowned the world in the time of Noah, the monster that swallowed Jonah, the Mediterranean tempest that shipwrecked St. Paul, and the dragon of the Apocalypse. In the *commedia* of the Bible, then, it is the anticomic monstrous power that controls most of the world until the Last Judgment, or whatever corresponds in the Bible to the comic recognition scene.

In the tempest comedies of Shakespeare there are recalls of most of these biblical associations. St. Paul's journeys are echoed in A *Comedy of Errors*, even in *The Tempest*. In *Pericles* the sailors' superstition that the ship will be wrecked if Thaisa's body is not thrown overboard suggests one of the adventures of Jonah, and the "caulked and bitumened" coffin that brings her safely to land suggests an ark. Antiochus, too, as the story of his death indicates, seems to be connected with the Antiochus of Syria who is one of the Antichrist figures of the Bible. In A *Comedy of Errors* the fear of the loss of identity, already referred to, is expressed in two or three images of sinking in water:

> I to the world am like a drop of water
> That in the ocean seeks another drop
> Who, falling there to find his fellow forth
> Unseen, inquisitive, confounds himself.

The feeling that in one dimension of the imagery we never quite get out of the sea recurs in *The Tempest*. In *The*

Merry Wives Mrs. Ford remarks, in exasperation, of Falstaff: "What tempest, I trow, threw this whale, with so many tuns of oil in his belly, ashore at Windsor?" We are reminded of the wife of Dromio of Ephesus, who takes Dromio of Syracuse to be her husband. Her horrified brother-in-law describes her as a monster whose body covers all Europe, and who is also full of oil: "If she lives till doomsday, she'll burn a week longer than the whole world."

In *The Tempest,* Prospero's magic is said to affect only the world of the four elements, his servants, including Ariel, being elemental spirits like the fairies of *A Midsummer Night's Dream.* This white magic is contrasted with the black magic of Sycorax, who has the traditional power of witchcraft over the moon, and, like Spenser's Mutability, threatens the whole cosmic order. Prospero can raise a tempest, like the witches in *Macbeth,* but his motives being good, his magic is in tune with the higher order of nature, and his last magical effort, just before he renounces his powers, is to "require" some heavenly music.

But although Prospero is benevolent and human, confining his work to the cycle of nature, the half of the cycle that he works in, the progress from death to renewed life, is an aspect of nature that still seems to us miraculous. The word "strange" is constantly echoed through the play, and Alonso opposes "strange" to natural, to be told by Prospero that what he thinks strange actually is natural. We notice that Prospero, in his renunciation speech, explicitly claims to have raised the dead, and the pretense that some of the characters

have actually died and come back to life is as strong as it is in
The Winter's Tale. Prospero pretends that he has lost Miranda "in this last tempest," and the mariners seem to be
spending the action of the play in a world of hellish music

> with strange and several noises
> Of roaring, shrieking, howling, jingling chains,
> And moe diversity of sounds, all horrible.

The island, then, is a place of confused identity in which a
world of nothingness, symbolized by the tempest and the sea,
separates from a world of regained identity in which Ferdinand receives a "second life" from Prospero, and the Court
Party, as Gonzalo says, find their true selves again. Stephano
and Trinculo fall into a "filthy-mantled pool" and Caliban is
persistently associated with fish: they hardly emerge from a
submarine world. The Court Party wander through a "maze"
of hallucinations, and for them the conceptions of reality
and illusion are reversed. In the *cognitio* Antonio and Sebastian understand that their realistic efforts to gain power by
assassination are what is unnatural, and so unreal, and that
the marvels and wonders of the magical island are a part of a
purgatorial cleansing of both their reason and their senses:

> And as the morning steals upon the night,
> Melting the darkness, so their rising senses
> Begin to chase the ignorant fumes that mantle
> Their clearer reason.

The higher or human nature which is revealed to them by
Prospero's art, an art including magic, music, and drama, is,

as Polixenes says in *The Winter's Tale*, an art which itself is nature. Polixenes, however, is thinking of this higher nature in the terms of a Renaissance highbrow: for him it is a conservative order, and belief in it is quite consistent with his going into a fury at the thought of his own stock being improved by the graft of a shepherd maiden. Perdita's repudiation of "bastard" flowers is not a hereditary nervousness about bastards: her chastity, as always in Shakespeare, is contained energy, and stands not for the purity of nature but for nature as a pulsating power, expressing itself in the miraculous springtime renewal which takes place without the aid of art.

/ The sense of the energy of nature is in *The Tempest* too: here again, as in *A Midsummer Night's Dream*, the fairies are instruments of energy and chastity, "pinching" the lazy and the dissolute. Prospero's magic is an identification with nature as a power rather than as an order or harmony, and is expressed in images of time rather than space, music rather than architecture. Like all magicians, he observes time closely ("The very minute bids thee ope thine ear," he says to Miranda), and his charms are effective only if he follows the rhythm of time. The subtitle of Greene's *Pandosto*, the source of the first part of *The Winter's Tale*, is "The Triumph of Time," and it is often suggested in the comedies that a power of bringing about the comic conclusion is inherent in time itself. From *Twelfth Night*, where Viola says: "O Time, thou must untangle this, not I!" to *The Winter's*

Tale, where Time is personified as the Chorus and speaks of his comic power

> To o'erthrow law and in one self-born hour
> To plant and o'erwhelm custom

we are aware of how deeply the spirit of magic and ritual, the sense of the significant act at the right time has been inherited by comic and romantic drama.

This feeling for the right time ramifies into all the imagery of *The Tempest*. The moon and the tides, several times mentioned in *The Winter's Tale* as well, in spite of the Mediterranean setting of both plays, are a part of its rhythm, and so is the moral virtue of patience, or waiting for the time to accomplish one's desires. Patience is one of the two virtues personified in the dialogue; the other is the "delicate wench" Temperance, the central virtue of all comedies, the etymology of which connects it, like the word tempest itself, with time (*tempestas*) and the distribution of time. The chastity of Miranda is a controlled energy that must develop from virginity to marriage by observing the proper rhythms of time and of ritual, otherwise the whole order of nature will go out of alignment. Prospero's concern on this point is a magical rather than a moral anxiety: the opposite pole is the incestuous daughter of Antiochus in *Pericles*, born at a most favorable time when "the senate-house of planets all did sit" and consequently very beautiful, but as Pericles says:

> being played upon before your time
> Hell only danceth at so harsh a chime.

The reference to music, an art dependent on time and rhythm, shows how essentially music and dance are involved in such imagery. We notice, too, how carefully the stage directions space out the movements in the masques and dumb shows.

Below this upper world of magic and music, which is also the world of genuine or restored nature, is the middle world of ordinary nature. This world is a cyclical movement between the poles of life and death, poles represented by the comic Eros and the tragic Thanatos or Adonis, Puck and Pyramus. In *A Midsummer Night's Dream* Cupid shoots an arrow at a "fair vestal" whose chastity makes her, like Miranda, part of the higher world of the moon and the music of the spheres. The arrow describes a parabola, which outlines, so to speak, the shape of the world it is in; it falls on a white flower and dyes it purple. The flower is called "love-in-idleness," and is used to inspire love, but purple is the color of the dying god, and the parabola movement was probably derived by Shakespeare from a curious image in Ovid's account of Pyramus. Another image of this cyclical world where life pursues death is the hunt, Diana the huntress being the earthly form of the moon goddess. The extraordinary loveliness of the lines given to Theseus and Hippolyta about the music of hunting suggest the harmony of a world below the heavenly sphere, theologically "fallen," but with its own kind of beauty and energy. *Twelfth Night* also begins with images of music, violets, and hunting inspired by love. In *Love's Labour's Lost* the killing of the deer by the princess is compared by Holofernes to an apple falling from heaven to earth: the image is deliberately absurd, and therefore contains something not wholly absurd. In *The Tempest* another fall under a tree, Stephano and Trinculo seizing the "glistering apparel" on the "line" (assuming that line here means linden tree) is immediately followed by their being hunted by spirits in the shapes of hounds. The *Twelfth Night* passage refers to the Actaeon myth, which naturally is central to this white-goddess cycle of love pursuing death, and the theme of wearing the horns of the deer in *As You Like It* and elsewhere may have more to do with this myth than with stale jokes about cuckolds. The identity of Eros and Adonis recurs in *The Winter's Tale*, where Perdita would like to strew Florizel with flowers, not "like a corse," but "like a bank for love to lie and play on."

Shakespeare frequently indicates the two poles of the natural cycle, in its various contexts, by a pair of songs. In *Love's Labour's Lost*, as mentioned earlier, we have the two songs of spring and winter, the order of which indicates the postponing of the comic conclusion. In *Cymbeline*, as also mentioned, there are the aubade and dirge of Imogen. In *The Winter's Tale* there might have been a winter song in the first part to contrast with Autolycus' song of the daffodils which begins the second, but a song would have been inappropriate in that part of the play. Its place is taken by the ghost story of the old man who dwelt by the churchyard, which Mamillius begins to tell. In *The Tempest* Ariel's first two songs of escape from and submergence in water, one a song of cocks and watchdogs and the other of funeral bells, have a similar contrast. The spirits addressed in the first song are those with "printless foot," referred to by Prospero, who keep on the shore just out of reach of the sea.

Prospero has been the expelled *idiotes* of a dramatic action that was completed fifteen years before the play begins. His position is not unlike Timon's to start with, but he has "books" and the kind of power symbolized by magic, which expresses itself very largely in music and drama. Timon, though he lives in a cave, is not a magician: he finds his gold by accident, and no suggestion of the supernatural is allowed to enter this particular play. The result is that, after trying to identify himself with the tempest world, with everything chaotic and destructive in nature, he finally dies "upon the beachèd verge of the salt flood." Prospero, in contrast, uses his magic to create what we have called a natural society out of the other characters. Because this natural society represents a higher order of nature than the one they know, what they get from him is a kind of initiation, like that of Aeneas in Virgil, whose journey the Court Party is repeating, as the dialogue about "widow Dido" and the identifying of Tunis with Carthage indicates. The opening tempest and the harpy banquet are other Virgilian echoes, rare as it is to find Shakespeare taking his eye off Ovid even for a few scenes. Gonzalo has some confused notion that a spiritual pilgrimage of some sort is going on: he sees the island as an earthly paradise and speaks of their fresh and new-dyed garments. But Antonio and Sebastian take longer to reach this point of view.

Prospero, with Ariel's help, divides the cast into three groups, corresponding roughly to the moral levels referred to earlier. First are the hero and heroine, Ferdinand and Miranda; next is the Court Party, including both the virtuous Gonzalo and the "three men of sin," and last are the group Caliban, Stephano, and Trinculo. Each of these goes through a typical ordeal. Ferdinand succeeds Caliban as a piler of logs; the Court Party wanders through "forthrights and meanders"; the clowns are submerged in a horsepond. Each, also, reaches an emblematic vision. Ferdinand and Miranda watch the masque of goddesses; the Court Party is introduced to the disappearing banquet. They have been brought up to think that reality is whatever their greed can clutch, and the disappearing banquet stands for the deceitful and illusory status of this kind of reality. Stephano and Trinculo are enticed to steal the glistering apparel dangled in front of them. These three visions are closely related to the three levels of the sheepshearing festival in *The Winter's Tale.* The masque of goddesses corresponds to Florizel's phrase "a meeting of the petty gods," with Perdita as Flora. Polixenes and Camillo, the spirits of the winter, came from the court to turn the festival into an illusion that they snatch away. Autolycus makes it an opportunity to steal purses and sell his bits of glistering apparel. He calls his stock "trumpery," the same word that Prospero uses to describe what he tempts Stephano and Trinculo with.

It is the wedding masque in which the dialectic of Shakespearean romance is most fully and completely stated. What the wedding masque presents is the meeting of earth and heaven under the rainbow, the symbol of Noah's new-washed world, after the tempest and flood had receded, and when it was promised that springtime and harvest would not cease. There is in fact a definite recall of the biblical scene:

> Spring come to you at the farthest
> In the very end of harvest.

But these lines say more: they say that out of the cycle of time in ordinary nature we have reached a paradise (Ferdinand's word), where there is a *ver perpetuum*, where spring and autumn exist together. It is not a timeless world, but it is a world in which time has a quite different relation to experience from ordinary time. Milton says of his Eden that there "spring and autumn/Danced hand in hand," and he may have been thinking of Shakespeare's masque, which ends in a dance of spring nymphs and autumn reapers. And because a new heaven and a new earth is a world of chastity and a recovery of innocence, Venus is expressly excluded from the masque. For Venus belongs to the cycle of life and death below this world, and wherever she is, "dusky Dis" is also.

With the vision of this world, the world of ordinary experience disappears, for the separation has finally been made between reality and illusion, the created and the objective. The world of what Pericles calls "a tempest,/A birth, and death," being finally expelled, becomes the world of non-being: we have only, in the words of *The Winter's Tale*, a world ransomed and a world destroyed. In the world of the masque time has become the rhythm of existence, the recovery by man of the energy of nature. In the nonexistent world below, time is the universal devourer that has finally nothing to swallow but itself. Prospero's great speech at the end of the masque tells us that everything we perceive disappears in this time. That is, the world of the spectator is ultimately abolished. What is presented to us must be possessed by us, as Prospero tells us in the Epilogue. We are told that the characters, as usual, will adjourn to hear more about themselves, but we need not follow them, for it is our own identity that we are interested in now. If anything is to make sense of this play, no less than of Peter Quince's play, it must be, as Hippolyta says, our imagination and not theirs. When Prospero's work is done, and there is nothing left to see, the vision of the brave new world becomes the world itself, and the dance of vanishing spirits a revel that has no end.

OTHER BOOKS ON DRAMA AVAILABLE IN PAPERBOUND
EDITIONS FROM HARCOURT, BRACE & WORLD, INC.

Plays

MAXWELL ANDERSON	Four Verse Plays (HB 25) (High Tor, Winterset, Elizabeth the Queen, Mary of Scotland)
ARISTOPHANES	Four Comedies (HB 51) *translated by Dudley Fitts* (Lysistrata, The Frogs, The Birds, Ladies' Day)
T. S. ELIOT	The Cocktail Party (HB 69)
	The Confidential Clerk (HB 70)
	The Family Reunion (HB 71)
	Murder in the Cathedral (HB 72)
DUDLEY FITTS, editor	Four Greek Plays (HB 33) (Agamemnon, Oedipus Rex, Alcestis, The Birds)
GÜNTER GRASS	Four Plays (HB 138)
	The Plebeians Rehearse the Uprising (HB 115)
MOLIÈRE	The Misanthrope and Tartuffe (HB 96) *translated by Richard Wilbur*
	Tartuffe (HB 130) *translated by Richard Wilbur*
SHAKESPEARE	Hamlet (H 001)
	King Henry the Fourth, Parts I and II (H 004)
	Macbeth (H 002)
	Twelfth Night (H 003)
SOPHOCLES	The Oedipus Cycle (HB 8) *translated by Dudley Fitts and Robert Fitzgerald*

Criticism

ERIC BENTLEY	The Playwright as Thinker (HB 123)
T. S. ELIOT	Essays on Elizabethan Drama (HB 18)
NORTHROP FRYE	Fables of Identity (H 035)

APR 2 0